CONTRACT LAW

FROM A

DRAFTING PERSPECTIVE

An Introduction to Contract Drafting
For Law Students

By

Thomas R. Haggard
Distinguished Professor of Law Emeritus
University of South Carolina
School of Law

AMERICAN CASEBOOK SERIES®

THOMSON
—✶—™
WEST

Mat #40116097

American Casebook Series and West Group are registered trademarks used herein under license.

ISBN 0–314–14449–8

TEXT IS PRINTED ON 10% POST CONSUMER RECYCLED PAPER

Dedicated
to my daughters

Kathrine Elizabeth Hudgins
and
Julie Gray Crowley

Who will perhaps
recognize some familiar
names and appreciate
the whimsey!

Table of Contents

Part II.
Additional Drafting Exercises

Preface

Drafted documents play a role in almost every area of the law. Yet, law school courses and casebooks rarely deal with the process and techniques for creating these documents. The focus, rather, is on substantive law.

This is especially true of the one course where a drafted document is involved in almost every case – contracts. First year contracts courses generally cover only the legal requirements of contract formation, enforcement of contracts, questions of interpretation, avoidance of contract duties, contract conditions, breach, third party beneficiaries, assignment and delegation, and remedies. Students attain an adequate mastery of the rules, doctrines, principles, theories, and social and economic policies that shape this area of the law. But students often come out of their contracts course with little if any knowledge or experience in the creation of contract documents.

Ironically, although good drafting is rarely taught, contracts students are exposed to massive doses of the bad variety. Many of the cases in a typical contracts text are there as a result of a failure in the drafting process. The contract thus led to expensive litigation rather than to a mutually satisfactory consummation of the transaction.

- For example, the frustration of purpose and impossibility of performance cases suggest that the drafter may not have adequately thought about the transaction, anticipated various possible occurrences, and dealt with them in the contract.

- Many of the parol evidence cases first year contracts students agonize over could have been avoided with an adequate merger clause in the contract.

- Cases that involve questions of contract interpretation usually arise because the drafter failed to use language that clearly and unequivocally expressed the intent of the parties.

- The liquidated damages cases nearly always involve a drafter's ignorance or disregard of the limits that the law imposes on this type of contract term.

- A large portion of third-party beneficiary law is designed to provide default rules for determining if the parties intended a particular person to be a third-party beneficiary, rules that were developed simply because the contract drafter failed to anticipate the possibility of a third-party beneficiary claim.

The mistakes of the drafter give courts the opportunity to create and explicate contract law theory, and that is what students learn. The purpose of this book is to take that learning process one step further by showing what a contract drafter might have done to avoid the problem in the first place. This will enable you, the student, to understand what contract law *really* means in the market place.

Part I. will introduce you to the process and techniques of contract drafting. Here, you will discover that thinking and planning are as integral to good drafting as are the purely linguistic skills. Indeed, without the former, the latter is largely a wasted effort.

Allow this portion of the text to stimulate your interest in drafting, not fully satisfy it. It is, at best, a highly abbreviated discussion of the principles and techniques that are covered in far greater detail in advanced drafting texts. Thus, if your school offers an upper-class course in either drafting generally or drafting in specific substantive areas (wills and estate planning, corporations, sales, real estate transactions, and others), by all means take advantage of the opportunity to improve your skills as a contracts drafter – because this text will not make you the expert that you need to be.

Part I. will also introduce you to the art of contract analysis and revision, as well as demonstrate how the drafter must always work with the statutory and common law of contracts well in mind.

Most of the chapters in Part I. include exercises that are designed to allow you to then apply what you have read about.

Part II. contains a variety of additional practical exercises. Some involve drafting specific provisions commonly found in commercial contracts. And some require you to draft an entire contract from scratch.

During my tenure at the University of South Carolina School of Law, I taught an advanced drafting course for many years, with a special emphasis on the techniques of contract drafting. When I taught first year contracts, I also incorporated a drafting component into that course. As a practitioner, I have drafted a fair number of contracts, of both the simple and complex variety. And, unfortunately, I have served as counsel in a number of contract lawsuits where bad drafting – in either the thinking or writing sense – was the true culprit. This book is the culmination of all those experiences. I hope it serves you well.

I want to thank the University of South Carolina School of Law for providing summer research money and release-time to work on this book. I also want to thank Kelly A. Wannamaker, USC School of Law, Class of 2003, for her invaluable research, editing, and proofreading assistance.

Thomas R. Haggard
Distinguished Professor of
Law Emeritus
University of South Carolina
School of Law
Columbia, SC 29208

September 2002

CONTRACT LAW
FROM A
DRAFTING PERSPECTIVE

An Introduction to Contract Drafting
For Law Students

Part I.
The Principles of Drafting

Chapter 1
Contract Law and the Role of the Contract Drafter

A. The Contract Drafter as a Private Legislator. When we hear the expression, *That's against the law,* we automatically think of conduct that violates some statutory provision – a federal law against discrimination, a state law requiring car occupants to wear seat belts, or a local ordinance prohibiting dogs from running loose. But when someone reneges on a promise to paint our house for $500, we call that *a breach of contract.*

Despite the different terminology and other distinctions, the two forms of conduct share one fundamental characteristic. Statutory provisions, which we call *public law*, are commands of the state requiring that we, the citizens, act or refrain from acting in certain ways, with non-compliance being punished with a variety of judicially imposed sanctions – prison terms, fines, civil penalties, disqualification from eligibility to participate in a benefit, and others. Contracts, which are called *private law*, also require the contracting parties to act or refrain from acting in certain ways, either absolutely or as a condition of entitlement. And when a contracting party fails to adhere to these requirements, the non-breaching party can call upon the coercive power of the state to obtain recompense – either in the form of damages or a court order to perform. Thus, the ultimate and overriding similarity between *public law* statutes and *private law* contracts is this: our refusal to pay a court-ordered fine imposed because we let our dog run loose and our refusal to pay court-awarded damages to our neighbor for the dog's miscreant behavior in digging up her flower bed will both ultimately have the same consequence – we will either act or refrain from acting as required by the statute or the agreement or the coercive power of the state will be brought to bear.

The functions and responsibilities of the *public law* drafter and the *private law* drafter are also similar in certain fundamental ways. The drafter of legislation, at the behest of our democratically elected officials, is attempting to reflect the will of the people regarding how we should act or refrain from acting. The drafter of contracts, on the other hand, at the behest of the client, is attempting to reflect the intent of the parties. In both instances, however, the accurate reflection and expression of the people's will or the parties' intent is an enormous responsibility, and sloppy drafting can have horrific consequences.

In sum, when you are drafting a contract, keep in mind that you are creating *law* that is going to bind people to act or refrain from acting in certain ways. True, the parties are expressly consenting to be bound in this fashion. But if the drafter fails to accurately reflect the intent of the parties and thus goes beyond their *actual* consent, they will still usually be bound – which is similar to a public law that is imposed by a non-democratic government. In this regard, the contract truly can be regarded as a *private legislator*.

B. The Contract Drafter as a Facilitator of Commerce. In a primitive economy, where goods and services are bartered and there is a direct and immediate exchange, contracts are unnecessary and contract drafters superfluous. Ours is not such an economy, and the material advantages that all of us enjoy would be impossible in the absence of contracts and a body of law that enforces those contracts. The complexity of our economy requires that the *promise* of a future exchange of goods and services be enforceable. A property owner promises to pay a contractor $100,000 for the construction of a house, and the contractor promises to build that house in a certain way. The owner would not be willing to pay that money in advance in the mere hope that the contractor would perform. And the contractor certainly would not be willing to build the house in the mere hope that the owner would pay.

A contract, consisting of promises that the law will enforce, is essential to a complex and flourishing economy. And it is the contract drafter who provides the substance of the contract to be enforced. If that contract is incomplete, if contingencies are not anticipated and dealt with, if the alleged contract does not contain the kind of promises that the law will enforce (supported by consideration), if the contract is so unclear that the parties cannot know what each other's rights and duties are, if certain provisions do not satisfy common law or statutory requirements, or if the parties contract on the basis of mistaken assumptions about the law or the facts, then the promises may either not be enforced at all or enforced on terms that at least one of the parties clearly did not subjectively consent to. When that happens, the driving force of an exchange economy is throttled.

The efficient and capable contract drafter prevents that from happening, drafts in such a way as to ensure that the agreed to exchange occurs without disputes or litigation, and thus plays a vital and necessary role in the economic system – as important as the owners of the capital equipment used to produced the goods or services exchanged, the workers who do the actual production, and the managers who coordinate the capital and labor resources.

So-called *transactional lawyers,* a fancy name for contract drafters, thus play a role in the legal system that is fundamentally different from that played by their more glamorous counterparts, the *litigators*. Litigators become involved only after something bad has happened – which, in the contract litigation context, usually means that the parties have a disagreement over what their respective rights and duties are under the contract. The litigator is hired to persuade the court that the interpretation given the contract by his or her client is the *correct* one, in that it accurately mirrors the intent of the parties at the time of contracting or because the client's position on a legal issue is supported by policy and precedent. As should be obvious by now, the function of the contract drafter is to do everything reasonably possible to prevent these disagreements from arising in the first place, so that the transaction will go through smoothly, efficiently, and harmoniously.

C. The Ethical Obligations of the Contract Drafter. The touchstone of drafting ethics is that the contract drafter is *acting on* *behalf of a client.* The contract drafter usually drafts on behalf of only one of the contracting parties. This is because lawyers have a duty of unqualified loyalty to their clients. That duty cannot be fulfilled if the attorney attempts to represent two clients with adverse interests. Certainly, an attorney could not represent the plaintiff in a tort action and also represent the defendant. This is called a *conflict of interests.*

Although a contract exchange will not even take place unless it is mutually beneficial, the parties have adverse or conflicting interests with respect to the specific terms of that exchange. A skillful and conscientious drafter on behalf of a seller will draft terms that benefit the seller, and one acting on behalf of a buyer would similarly represent that client. It is thus difficult, if not impossible, for the same lawyer to represent both buyer and seller. Indeed, the only situations in which this would be permissible involve very simple transactions, where the parties have already reached an agreement over terms, and where all they need is a lawyer to put this agreement into written contract form. But even here the lawyer must be satisfied that the terms are compatible with the best interest of both parties and that the lawyer can be impartial in the performance of the drafting assignment. If, after reviewing the terms of the agreement, the lawyer determines that the contract will not be fair to one of the parties, the lawyer must decline to draft the document and suggest that both parties retain separate attorneys to advise them on this matter.

The interests of the client also require that the drafter be competent and diligent. Drafters have been found guilty of ethical violations, and subject to malpractice claims, for drafting provisions that do not satisfy statutory requirements, for drafting an ambiguous provision that was resolved against the client, for a failure to include certain provisions beneficial to the client, and for other acts of incompetence and sloth. Following the drafting processes and techniques discussed in this book will help you avoid this kind of error.

Attorney fees are a ready source of client complaint, and the attorney has a number of ethical obligations in this regard. One that is of particular concern to the drafter is the requirement that the fee accurately reflect the nature and value of the services rendered. A real estate attorney who has spent sixteen hours drafting a lease agreement for a large apartment complex can legitimately bill the client on an hourly basis. The attorney is also entitled to use this document as a model when drafting on behalf of another apartment owner. Indeed, only minor changes may be necessary. The attorney may not, however, claim to have spent another sixteen hours on this document and bill on that basis. Nor is the attorney limited to billing for the one additional hour that was spent making the necessary revisions. Rather, instead of billing on a hourly basis at all, the attorney can adopt a *value billing* approach and charge a flat fee for this service, as long as this is understood in advance by the client.

The attorney's ethical duty of confidentiality is also of special importance to contract drafters. Often, the details of an anticipated transaction must remain secret until it is *a done deal*. For example, if a developer has an option contract on a particular piece of land, public knowledge of this would seriously inflate the price of neighboring pieces of land that the developer is also attempting to obtain option contracts on. It would be a serious breach of ethics for the attorney to leak this information – or to allow anyone in the attorney's office to do so!

Although the wording of the ethical rules on this vary and the meaning of those rules is uncertain in many drafting contexts, it is generally unethical for an attorney to draft a contract that involves a criminal, illegal, or fraudulent transaction. Clearly, one could not draft a contract for the sale of crack cocaine. One could not draft a contract for the sale of a Monet painting that is actually a reproduction, since this is fraudulent. Fraud, however, is a slippery concept and it is not always easy to distinguish true *fraud* from what is merely *sharp dealing*.

Drafting contract provisions that are *illegal* only in the sense that they are unenforceable may also be unethical, especially if they are being used by one party to exploit the ignorance of the other. For example, a landlord may want to include lease provisions that impose duties on a tenant that cannot be enforced under the state landlord-tenant law or purport deprive the tenant of rights guaranteed by that statute. Out of ignorance, the tenant may perform the duties or forgo the exercise of rights. Under the statute, these provisions are simply *void*, not affirmatively *illegal* in the sense that the landlord will be subject to civil or criminal penalties for including them in the lease. But, whether strictly prohibited by the canons of ethics or not, the conscientious lawyer should refrain from drafting these provisions.

Finally, the ethical rules prohibit or limit the attorney-drafter from entering into contract transactions with clients. For example, an attorney cannot enter into a business deal with a client unless the terms of the contract are fair and the client has had the opportunity to consult with other counsel. Similarly, the terms of the retainer agreement between the attorney and the client are subject to several requirements – such as the requirement of a written agreement if the representation is on a contingent fee basis.

Some of the Exercises in Part II. of this book will raise these and other ethical concerns.

Chapter 2
The Drafting Process

Drafting involves far more than mere writing. It is an intellectually demanding, creative, problem-solving process, the end result of which only happens to be a written document. This process involves several discrete functions. They all have one objective – the creation of a document that satisfies the client's needs. Pragmatically, this means structuring a transaction that goes through smoothly, resulting in neither hard feelings between the parties nor litigation.

The various things that a drafter must do before even attempting to write can be summarized as follows:

A. Ask *Why?* The client has asked you to draft a particular kind of contract. But a piece of paper with words on it is not what the client wants. The document is merely the means to an end. To draft effectively, the drafter must know the client's ultimate goal, objective, or purpose.

In most cases, this is fairly obvious from the nature of the contract itself. If the client wants a contract for the sale of residential property, the client's need is to obtain a binding commitment from another person to buy or sell the property so that, at a later date, title and possession will pass from one party to the other.

But suppose the client suddenly decides that he or she needs to have a written employment contract with the company's Director of Research and Development. Apparently, something has happened that created the client's perception of a need. Perhaps a problem has arisen that the client thinks can be solved or avoided in the future with a written contract. To draft a contract that achieves this client's goals, the drafter must know what happened and what the problem is. Otherwise, the drafter could produce an otherwise exemplary employment contract, but it would not be one that solved or forestalled the problem. Such a contract would be the result of bad drafting – not in the literary sense, but in the intellectual sense.

B. Identify the Audience. The so-called *audience* to a contract refers to those individuals, other than the client, who will read or use the contract for some reason. The lawyer must draft with this audience in mind – know who they are, what characteristics they possess, and how they will use the document.

The most proximate member of this audience is, of course, the other actual or potential party to the contract. This other contracting party may be in one of several postures at the time the contract is drafted. First, the client and the other party may have already negotiated and orally agreed to the terms of the contract, with the written version merely serving as a tangible memorial. The drafter's duty here is to reflect that oral agreement as closely as possible. Having done that, the drafter may want to suggest that the client propose certain modifications to their agreed-upon contract.

Second, the client and the other party may have generally or tentatively agreed to the transaction, but without intending yet to be bound and leaving the details to be worked out in the written contract. Here, the drafter should adhere to the broad contours of the agreement, but should feel free to advance the client's interests when drafting the details.

Third, the other party's status may simply be that of a potential offeree. The client is going to use the written contract primarily as an offer. Here, the drafter must recognize that further negotiation is probably anticipated. The document, thus, should contain some provisions that the client is willing to give up (barter material), but should not be so one-sided as to cause the offeree to reject the proposal out of hand or justify a court in later voiding a provision for being unconscionable.

The drafter must also take the other party's status or characteristics into account. If the other party is a member of a class to which the law affords special protection – consumers, for example – then this offer/contract must scrupulously avoid overreaching and may even have to satisfy certain statutory *readability* requirements.

Sometimes, the other party to the contract may be a *reader in bad faith*. This refers to someone who, if any minuscule advantage is to be gained from it, will exploit every loophole, pounce on any ambiguity, and construe any vagueness in his or her favor. Honoring contract obligation is not a moral imperative to this person. Rather, honoring or dishonoring contract obligations is simply an economic decision, measuring the risks and costs of litigation against burdens and inconvenience of performance. If you are dealing with that kind of contracting party, then you need to draft with special care.

Conversely, if the party with whom your client is contracting is an old friend or business associate, then the drafter can structure the transaction more loosely, relying on the good faith of the parties to work out any disagreements over detail or meaning. Caveat: There have been some pretty nasty lawsuits over contracts between "*former* friends." So do not get too casual.

Although the other party to a contract is the primary audience of a drafted contract, this person is not the only audience. A contract between two corporations for the sale and purchase of assets will be read and used for many different purposes by a variety of people: stockholders, numerous regulatory agencies (each with its own agenda), banks, financial analysts, unions representing employees, creditors, potential assignees, newspaper reporters, and others.

Finally, the ultimate audience of a contract may be a judge or arbitrator. Although litigation is usually the result of bad drafting, this is not always so. For a variety of reasons, the best of contracts sometimes end up in litigation. The drafter should anticipate this possibility and deal with it. For example, judges tend to be hostile to seemingly harsh provisions that favor the contracting party with the so-called *superior bargaining power*. The drafter of such a provision should use conciliatory language, go no further than the client's interests actually require, and perhaps even explain the purpose of the provision within the contract itself.

C. Understand the Broader Factual Context. Contracts never function in hermetically sealed isolation. The contract drafter must know as much as possible about the factual context in which the contract will be performed. If a certain drafter had known, for example, that two ships named *Peerless* were scheduled to sail from Bombay in the fall and winter in a certain year in the early 1860s, then the intended ship would have been identified and the fatal ambiguity that defeated the contract in the famous case of *Raffles v. Wichelhaus* would have been avoided. Similarly, all contracts are drafted against a background of certain tacit assumptions, business practices, and vocabularies that may attach a meaning to a word that differs from the ordinary dictionary definition.

The more that is known about all of these matters, the better able the drafter will be in avoiding difficulties for the client.

D. Determine What Should Be In the Contract. This usually stops first year law students (and many young lawyers!) dead cold. The client wants a contract for the sale of residential property. But what should the document contain? What, if anything, does the law require? What factual aspects of the transaction need to be dealt with to ensure that everything goes smoothly? These are not easy questions to answer.

The legal requirements can be discovered through research. The factual aspects are more troublesome. The drafter may know what to include because the drafter is familiar with this kind of business transaction and is sensitive to the *friction points* that will require attention. A contract for the sale of a house should, for example, clarify the status of those items the buyer may assume go with the house – drapes, shades, or window air conditioning units – while the seller assumes otherwise.

Alternatively, the neophyte drafter may resort to legal form books to determine the appropriate content of a particular kind of contract. The best thing about these books is often not the language they suggest for specific provisions (which is usually atrocious), but rather the factual checklists they contain.

All else failing, the drafter can fall back on the technique reporters follow when investigating news stories. Identify the relevant *who, what, when, where, how,* and *why* with respect to every aspect of the transaction. If a contract covers all of this information, it is likely to be factually comprehensive. For example, consider the factual elements of this simple contract.

Who? The parties are Sally Seller and Bill Buyer. But the contract also calls for binding arbitration. Who is the arbitrator going to be? That is a critical component of the contract.

What? The transaction is a sale. The object is a priceless book, the first edition of *Contract Law From A Drafting Perspective.* The price is $500.00.

When? The exchange of money and book will take place next Tuesday; the contract is being signed today.

Where? The exchange will occur in the Student Lounge on the third floor.

How? Seller will bring the book in person, still in its sealed plastic sleeve. Buyer will pay with a certified check.

Why? The drafter has already dealt with this at the initial stage of the enquiry, and the *why* of a transaction usually does not need to appear within the contract itself. Sometimes, however, it does. When included within the preamble of a contract, an explanation of the purpose of the transaction may assist the court in construing the contract or in determining damages. The Seller/Buyer contract, for example, might explain that Buyer needs the book to complete a collection of books that will be worth considerably more with this addition than it would without it. If a preamble contains this information, it could be used to establish

Buyer's damages in case of breach or even provide the justification for a decree of specific performance.

These sources and techniques will at least provide the drafter with the essential elements of the contract, enough to keep the document from being declared unenforceable because of incompleteness. But the competent drafter can never be satisfied with the bare minimum. Based on the drafter's understanding of the factual context in which this contract will operate, the drafter must ask a relentless series of *what if* questions. *What if your client is unable to meet the delivery schedule because of snow? What if the buyer's need for widgets, which your client is promising to meet for the next three years, later increases dramatically, taxing your client's ability to keep its promise? What if the wedding is called off and the bride no longer needs the reception hall? What if the reception hall burns down? What if while digging you hit a layer of hard rock instead of the sand you expected, increasing your excavation costs by 200%? What if the other contracting party decides that she wants to assign her rights under the contract to a third party, whether your client likes it or not?*

No one, of course, can anticipate every eventuality. At some point, even attempting to do so will increase the drafting costs beyond what is reasonable. And if it is theoretically possible, but highly unlikely, that something is going to happen, then there may be no need to try to deal with it in the contract. Indeed, negotiations over the whole contract may fail because the parties cannot agree on how some remote eventuality should be dealt with. Here, it is better either to assume that the parties will be able to work out the difficulty, if it arises, or simply fall back on the contract law default rules, even if their application is uncertain at the time of contracting.

E. Check the Law. The contract drafter must always draft within the constraints of both common and statutory law. A plaintiff forced to overcome the defense of *nudum pactum* by convincing the court that the plaintiff's duties or constraints are implied in the contract could have avoided that difficulty if the drafter had been more sensitive to the common law requirement of consideration and expressly provided for it in the document. Some contract provisions would be unenforceable because they are unconscionable. The Uniform Commercial Code imposes certain requirements on contract provisions that purport to disclaim warranties. State and federal laws also impose other complicated limits and requirements on contracts dealing with apartment leases, insurance, securities, employment, transportation, and other specialized areas.

F. Conceptualize. Concepts, which are the mental images of reality, possess three sets of somewhat overlapping and related characteristics or variables. They provide the drafter with three sets of fundamental choices.

- Specificity/generality.

- Precision/vagueness.

- Concreteness/abstraction.

By making the correct choices between these three sets of alternatives, the drafter can craft a document that serves the client's needs effectively and efficiently.

1. Specificity/Generality. *A Boxer/Labrador mix named Nemo* is a very specific entity encompassed by the larger generality of *dog*, which itself is encompassed by the even larger generality of *animal*. The drafter must identify the client's goals or objectives by reference to the proper level of specificity or generality. Does the client want a contract for the sale of Nemo specifically? Or would the client be content for the contract to be for the sale of any dog? Or any animal? Finding the right level of specificity/generality ensures that the contract is neither under- nor over-inclusive of the client's objectives.

2. Precision/Vagueness. Contract terms can be precise, as in *24 hours*, or they can be vague, as in *a reasonable* *time*. Precise terms have fixed, easily identified boundaries. We know exactly when the 24-hour limit is exceeded. Vague terms are fuzzy at the border. Whether a *reasonable time* has expired will nearly always depend on the nature of the contract and the circumstances.

The advantage of precision is that it leaves little room for disagreement, thus avoiding costly litigation. Over-precision, however, is also dangerous because it locks the parties into a straight-jacket of rights and duties. If the contract requires seller to do A, B, and C, then that is exactly what the seller must do if the buyer insists on it, even if it turns out later that D would be a perfectly reasonable alternative to C – and one that a vague term would have allowed seller to pursue.

In contrast, vagueness builds some flexibility into the transaction. It provides a cushion against unexpected and unforeseeable circumstances. It allows the contracting parties to focus on the important terms during negotiations rather than getting bogged down over minutia. And it is usually easier to resolve later disagreements over vague terms than it is to convince someone that a precisely worded provision really should not be read so literally.

There are, however, also some dangers inherent in vagueness. A vague term may be the source of legitimate disagreement later on. Certainly, vagueness should be avoided if the drafter suspects that the other party to the contract is likely to be a *reader in bad faith*. Vagueness should also be distinguished from ambiguity, which will be discussed in Chapter 4.

3. Concreteness/Abstraction. A concrete term deals with something that you can actually see, hear, smell, or feel – a tangible object, such as *a pillow*. An abstract term deals with a quality or result, such as *soft*. Draft in terms of what the client really wants. Is it truly a pillow? Or will anything soft do just as well?

Drafting in terms of an abstraction is often necessary when the client knows generally what effect he or she wants to achieve, such as a garden area suitable for entertaining large crowds, but has no grasp of or is indifferent to the details or particulars of such a garden. The contract, thus, could be drafted in terms of this overall objective, leaving the details to the landscaper's discretion. Needless to say, this presumes that the client has faith in the judgment and skill of the landscaper. And the landscaper always runs the risk of the client saying later, "This isn't what I had in mind at all!"

Exercise # 1 – Conceptual Alternatives.

1. In a contract for the installation of a wooden deck on the back of a house, which level of generality/specificity would *probably* be the most appropriate? Why?

- Pine planks.
- Pressure treated according to USDA standards 2 x 6 pine planks.
- Pressure treated according to USDA standards 2 x 6 pine planks manufactured and distributed by the Oregon Lumber Company.

2. Suppose that the home owner in the deck contract has proposed a term prohibiting the contractor from doing the work, which is quite noisy, at *unreasonable* hours. Why might the contractor object to the wording? Propose something that might be more satisfactory.

3. The proposed contract provides that the deck will be *stained with a waterproof stain in a color that is compatible with the house*, which is a natural cedar. That contracts in terms of a desired result, and is thus an abstraction. What would be a more concrete alternative?

G. Organize. The drafter knows what the client expects the document to achieve, who will be using the document and how, what the substantive content will be, the legal constraints, and how this substance is going to be conceptualized. The next step is to get all of this organized.

Ordinarily, contracts should be written in outline form, with numbered or lettered headings that identify the substance of each provision. This makes it easier for readers to find and refer to the various substantive terms. For example, a section of an employment contract might look like this:

> *VII. Compensation*
> > *A. Base Salary*
> > *B. Overtime*
> > *C. Incentive Pay*
> > *D. Discretionary Bonuses*

Other drafters prefer to use section designations, as follows:

> *Section 7 -- Compensation*
> > *§ 7-1 Base Salary*
> > *§ 7-2 Overtime*
> > *§ 7-3 Incentive Pay*
> > *§ 7-4 Discretionary Bonuses*

Organization consists of three related elements – division, classification, and sequence.

1. Division. Division consists of breaking the mass of data into categories and subcategories. Division is subject to three rules.

First, parallel categories should be mutually exclusive, so that a particular provision can be placed in one category or another, but not both. This is not always possible, but it does simplify the classification task. Similarly, if the categories purport to be parallel or at the same level of hierarchy, as in *A, B, C*, then this rule of division is violated if *B* is in fact merely a component or subcategory of *A*. For example, in an employment contract, one should not have a category called *A. Compensation* and also one called *B. Commissions*, since the latter is itself a form of compensation and should be listed under *A*, along with the other forms of compensation.

Second, the sum of the subcategories must equal the category. In the above example, base salary, overtime, incentive pay, and discretionary bonuses must represent the entire compensation package. If, later in the contract, you have a provision dealing with sales commissions, then you have breached this rule of division.

Third, if practicable, division should be based on one principle. In a contract for the sale of goods, the goods in question could be divided on the basis of color or weight, but not both simultaneously.

Consider how a division of your *Law School* into *A. first year law students* and *B. female law students* violates all three rules. Being a first year law student is not mutually exclusive of being a female law student, thus violating rule one. Where would you classify Sarah Elizabeth, a first-year, female law student? The suggested division also violates the second rule, since the law school community consists of more than first year students and female law students; it also includes second and third year men, faculty members, and others. Where would they be placed in this divisional scheme? And the division is based both on class and sex, violating the third rule.

2. Classification. Classification consists of assigning specific provisions to the proper category. No matter how careful the drafter is, no division is absolutely air-tight. Where to put a particular provision is thus subject to some judgment. For example, an apartment lease might have one provision entitled *Security Deposit* and another entitled *Termination*. The landlord's right to retain some of the security deposit to pay for repairs and duty to return the rest of it could rationally be included in the *Security*

Deposit provision, together with the amount and the tenant's duty to pay. Or it could be included in the *Termination* section, together with other matters relating to the rights and duties of the parties at end of the lease period. The controlling principle is this: Put a provision into the category where the readers of the contract are most likely to look for it.

3. Sequence. Sequence refers to the order in which the provisions of the contract are presented. The following is a fairly traditional sequence.

Introductory Paragraph. Most contracts begin with an unnumbered and un-captioned introductory paragraph that identifies the parties, sometimes indicates the nature of the contract, and contains the critical *mutually agree* language to satisfy the consideration requirement.

CONTRACT OF SALE

> *Thompson Seedless Grape Co, Inc. (Seller) and Nubbin Sales, Inc. (Buyer) enter into this contract for the sale of grapes and mutually agree to the following terms and conditions.*

Recitals. This is sometimes followed by a recitals section, often captioned *Background*. A recitals section may used for several purposes:

- To explain the purpose of the contract, which might be useful later if a *frustration of purpose* issue arose.

- To state a mutual understanding of fact, which would be relevant if a *mistake* issue arose.

- To provide background information that could be relevant in computing damages, such as a statement of the seller's sales volume over the last several years.

- To explain why a *time is of the essence* clause should be strictly enforced.

- To neutralize the apparent harshness of a contract term by explaining the need for it, thus avoiding a later claim of unconscionability.

Some courts have said that recitals are not part of the contract. This is incorrect. They are indeed a part of the contract, but differ from the remainder of it in that recitals are not promissory in form and thus do not create rights and duties. They do, however, establish the factual predicate of the contract, and some courts have held that facts contained in a recital are not subject to disproof in a trial. Recitals, thus, can have enormous legal significance.

Formerly, recitals were often introduced with *WHEREAS*. This is archaic legalese. Say what you want to say in plain English.

Definitions. If a contract is going to define the terms it uses throughout the document, this section should come next. If, however, the contract is long and complex and a specific term is going to be used in only one section, it may be better to define that term within the section in question, so the reader does not have to go back to the beginning of the document to find out what the term means. Definitions are discussed in Chapter 5.

Substantive Provisions. The substantive provisions of the contract can be organized in a number of ways. To some extent, this is dictated by the scheme of division the drafter has adopted. Among the major divisional categories and the individual provisions within each, many drafters prefer to follow a chronological sequence.

Housekeeping Provisions. These are provisions that relate to the administration and enforcement of the contract. They typically include provisions relating to severability, choice of law, modification, no waiver of rights, merger, assignment, delegation, survivability, notices, liquidated damages, force majeure, and other matters. Sometimes, if they are particularly complicated, provisions relating to damages and the availability of injunctive relief are put in their own major category.

Signatures and Date. The persons who sign the contract will normally be bound by it. Drafters must take care when dealing with someone who might be a minor or lacks contractual capacity because of a mental state. If the intent is to bind a business entity, then the drafter should ensure that the person signing the contract on behalf of the entity has the authority to do so.

Notarization and Witnesses. Unless it is required by statute, a contract need not be notarized or witnessed. Although some drafters think this impresses the parties with the legal significance of what they are doing, most drafters regard it as meaningless window dressing.

Exercise # 2 – Organization. Organize these specific contract provisions in a logical fashion. Create numbered and titled headings and subheadings and list the # of each provision that would go under these headings and subheading. This will be a tri-party construction contract between an Owner, a Contractor, and an Architect. The following merely indicates the topic of the provision, not necessarily its full and final wording.

> #1   Contractor will build the structure according to the attached plans and specifications.
>
> #2   At the completion of construction, Architect will inspect the work within 24 hours following notification of completion by the Contractor.
>
> #3   Owner will pay $1,500 upon the beginning of construction.

#4   At the completion of construction, Contractor will remove all debris, tools, and equipment from the site within four days.

#5   If the work complies with the plans and specifications, Architect will sign a Certificate of Compliance and present it to the Owner.

#6   Owner will provide electrical power to the site.

#7   Before beginning construction, Contractor will post a performance and indemnity bond in the amount of $10,000.

#8   Upon receipt of Architect's Certificate of Compliance, Owner will pay Contractor an additional $2,000.

#9   When determining whether Contractor has complied with the plans and specification, Architect will exercise good faith and evaluate the work in accordance with established building practices and procedures.

#10   Owner will make reasonable efforts to prevent any third party access to the construction site while work is in progress.

#11   Contractor will pay all subcontractors and materialmen promptly upon demand or as the contracts between these parties provide.

#13   Contractor will carry Workers' Compensation Insurance on everyone who Contractor employs directly.

#14   Owner will indemnify Contractor for any liability that Contractor incurs as a result of injury to third parties (other than subcontractor or materialmen) who, despite Owner's best efforts to prevent it, enter the construction site while work is in progress.

#15   If the Architect determines that the work is not in compliance with the plans and specifications or is not in accordance with established building practices and procedures, Architect will present Contractor with a written list of defects and provide Owner with a copy.

#16   Contractor will not work on the site before 8:00 a.m., after 7:00 p.m., or on Sunday.

#17   Contractor will not engage any subcontractor to work on the site without first obtaining a written assurance that the subcontractor carries Workers' Compensation insurance on its employees.

#18   If, after inspecting the work, the Architect provides Contractor with a written list of defects, Contractor will cure these defects within seven days.

#19   Owner, Contractor, and Architect will resolve any otherwise unresolved disputes that arise under this contract by submitting the dispute to an arbitrator selected by the State Arbitration & Mediation Service.

#20   Contractor will use only materials that are certified as "Made in America."

#21   Contractor will compensate its employees in compliance with the federal Fair Labor Standards Act and the State Wage Payment Statute.

#22   Owner, Contractor, and Architect will do nothing to impede or interfere with any other party's performance of this contract.

H. Write. *Finally!*, you might think. This, however, only illustrates that drafting is as much a thinking and planning exercise as it is a writing exercise – if not more so. Indeed, the writing phase of drafting is perhaps the easiest to learn and to perform.

Linguistically, the drafter needs to do five things.

● Adopt a style that is clear, simple, and concise.

● Avoid ambiguity.

● Be careful when creating definitions.

● Use the proper terms to create various legal consequences.

● Draft with the so-called *Canons of Interpretation* in mind.

These aspects of the writing/drafting process will be discussed in the next five chapters.

I. Review, Revise, and Edit the Document. Contract drafters frequently quit too early. As soon as the document comes out of the printer, it is stuffed into an envelope with a cover letter and dispatched to the client. This is an invitation to disaster. The drafter must take the time to revisit all of the planning steps. If what the drafter has written is, upon thoughtful review, found to be discongruant with what the client wants and needs, then substantive revision is necessary. Having previously focused primarily on substance and organization, the drafter can now address matters of style. And finally, typographical errors, which inevitably and insidiously creep in during the last minute substantive revisions, can be eliminated with one final proofreading – best done by someone other than the drafter! Then, and only then, is the drafting process complete.

Chapter 3
Drafting Style and Usage

Drafted documents do not need to be eloquent. But they do need to be clear, simple, and concise.

A. Clarity. Above everything else, the parties to the contact need to understand what they are agreeing to, and this must also be apparent to the other audiences of the contract – the courts, most especially.

Ambiguity, which will be discussed in more detail in Chapter 4, is the very antithesis of clarity. Consider the offer to sell a *little used sailboat*. Assume that the offeror owns two sailboats, one that is small and the other that has been in the water only one summer. Which is being sold? True, the absence of a comma indicates that *little* modifies *used.* But a hyphen should have been used if that was the intent. The phrase is thus ambiguous enough that a court would probably allow extrinsic evidence of its intended meaning. This is not the result the drafter should strive for.

Of course, a document may be lacking in clarity even if it is not literally ambiguous. Convoluted sentence structure, poor organization, and a host of other defects can contribute to the opaqueness of a document.

B. Simplicity. A drafted document should not be like a nineteenth century Victorian house, with gingerbread trim, filigrees, turrets, and multiple roof angles. Rather, it should be cubical, with right angle lines, clean and uncluttered by features that perform no function.

C. Concision. Being concise is not the same as being brief. Brevity relates to length in an absolute sense, whether the document adequately serves the needs of the client or not. A one-page contract may be brief, but inadequate to the task. Concision, in contrast, relates to saying what *needs* to be said in the fewest words possible. A 50 page contract, though not brief, may be concise.

D. The Conventions of Style and Usage That Promote Clarity, Simplicity, and Concision.

1. Use Consistent Terminology. Always use the same word to refer to the same person, thing, entity, or concept. Always use different words to refer to different persons, things, entities, and concepts. A reader will only be confused if the object of the sale is variously referred to as the *car, vehicle, automobile,* and *item.* Similarly, if you have once used the term *automobile* to refer to the new car that is being purchased, do not use the same term to refer to the trade-in car. When selecting a shorthand designation for a contracting party, select only one – *Crowley Engineering Co., Inc. ("Builder"),* not *("Crowley" or "Builder").*

2. Write Short Sentences. Limit each sentence to one idea. Deliver the substance of the document to the reader one bite at a time. Aim for an average sentence length of 20 words. Unless the sentence contains a list, a date, or an address, any sentence with more than two commas in it is probably too long. This suggests that the sentence is either compound (two grammatical sentences joined by *and*) or complex (packed with subordinate clauses and phrases). They should be expressed in separate sentences.

For example, this compound/complex sentence is too long:

Buyer, who will make all shipment arrangements, will accept the goods at the place of delivery, which is Seller's plant in Ohio, and will have the goods removed by no later than 10 days following the date of this contract, subject to extension if Department of Transportation permits are delayed. [50 words]

It could be broken down, reworded, and condensed as follows:

Buyer will accept delivery of the goods at Seller's plant in Ohio. Within 10 days following the date of this contract, Buyer will remove the goods from Seller's premises. [Being responsible for making the shipment arrangements is implicit.] *This time is automatically extended if Department of Transportation permits are delayed.* [13words average]

3. Use Simple Sentence Structure. The easiest type of sentence for the reader to comprehend is one that is structured in order of subject, verb, and object. *Seller and Buyer* [subject] *agree* [verb] *to the following terms and conditions* [object]. In a memorandum or brief, this would give the document a *see Dick run* simplicity and monotony, and one would want to vary the sentence structure accordingly. But this is not a problem in a drafted document; it is expected to be functional, not eloquent.

4. Use Common, Ordinary Words. Literary writers often use a Thesaurus to find the fanciest word possible. Drafters should use a Thesaurus in just the opposite direction. If you have referred to *the contiguous property* in a contract, run *contiguous* through the Thesaurus on your computer and replace it with *adjoining.* Similarly,

- Say *sign* instead of *execute.*
- Say *use* instead of *utilize.*
- Say *debt* instead of *indebtedness.*
- Say *pay* instead of *remunerate.*

Words ending in *-ee* and *-or*, like *vendee* and *vendor*, should be replaced with less confusing designations, like *buyer* and *seller.* *Lessor* and *lessee* are particularly confusing. Say *landlord* (or *owner*) and *tenant.* Likewise, unless it is a true term of art, replace foreign words and phrases, like *fructus fundi*, with their more common English counterpart, *produce of the land.*

5. Use Terms of Art and Trade Terms Consciously and Cautiously. Each area of the law has its own terms of art and trade words – words and phrases that have an often complex, relatively fixed, but usually unconventional meaning. They can pose a trap for the unwary drafter. In the lumber business, for example, a 2 by 4 is not literally 2 inches by 4 inches. And who would have thought that the word *chicken* includes "boiler or fryer . . . , roaster . . . , capon . . . , stag . . . , hen or stewing chicken or fowl . . . , [and] cock or old rooster"?[1]

6. Avoid Unconventional Capitalization. In addition to words at the beginning of a sentence, capitalize only proper nouns and their shorthand designations, like *Hudgins Environmental Services, Inc. (Consultant)*. Putting introductory or important words, like *THEREFORE* or *ALL LATE PAYMENTS,* in all-caps is distracting and should be avoided unless required by statutory conspicuousness requirements.

7. Eradicate All Legalese. Perhaps nothing makes drafted documents so pompous-sounding and incomprehensible to lay readers as the use of archaic terms like *aforementioned, hereinabove, hereinafter, thenceforth, whensoever, wheresoever, whereas, witnesseth,* and the like.

Probably the most obnoxious form of contract document legalese is the heading that still appears on some commercially prepared form contracts.

KNOW ALL MEN BY THESE PRESENTS:

This is sexist, archaic, and no one has any idea what it means.

8. Avoid the Use of *said, such,* and *same*. Do not use *said* or *such* as adjectives. Replace *said goods* and *such goods* with *the goods*. Do not use *such* or *same* as pronouns. Repeat whatever the antecedent noun is. Replace *and will ship same* with *will ship the tractor*.

---

[1] See *Frigaliment Importing Co. v. B.N.S. International Sales Corp.*, 190 F. Supp. 116 (S.D.N.Y. 1960).

9. Never Use *and/or*. In addition to being ambiguous, this term has received more judicial opprobrium than almost any term in the drafting lexicon.   One judge described it as "that befuddling, nameless thing, that Janus-faced monstrosity, neither word nor phrase, the child of a brain of someone too lazy to express his precise meaning, or too dull to know what he did mean, now commonly used by lawyers in drafting legal documents, through carelessness or ignorance or as a cunning device to conceal rather than express meaning with view to furthering the interests of their clients."[2]

10. Eliminate All Redundant Couplets and Triplets. Contracts are often larded with expressions like:

- *furnish and supply*
- *sell, alienate, and dispose of*
- *terminate, cancel, or revoke*
- *lien, charge, or encumbrance*

Replace these wordy twofers and threefers with a single term, choosing the one that is simplest and most common.

11. Eliminate Redundant Enumeration. Perhaps the silliest thing contract drafters do is express numbers in both Arabic and by spelling them out. It is unnecessary to say that *Seller has four (4) days to notify Buyer of delivery*. Adopt a convention of when to use Arabic (1 through 9, for example) and when to spell out. Adhere to it throughout the contract.

12. Omit *the fact that*. Instead of saying:

The fact that the buyer failed to inspect the goods constitutes waiver.

---

[2] *Employers' Mut. Liab. Ins. Co. v. Tollefsen*, 263 N.W. 376, 377 (Wisc. 1935).

Say:

The buyer's failure to inspect the goods constitutes waiver.

13.   Eliminate Other Redundant Expressions.
Implicit in the notion of *100 yards* is that a *distance* is involved. It is thus unnecessary to refer in a contract to *a distance of 100 yards.*
Similarly:

- Omit *period* in *after a period of a week.*
- Omit *the month of* in *during the month of October.*
- Omit *until a later time* in *postponed until a later time.*

14.   Eliminate Unnecessary Words, Phrases, and Sentences. Every word and collection of words in a contract must carry its own weight and contribute something essential to the mission of the document. If words can be eliminated without altering the substance or clarity of the contract (for example, where the substance has already been dealt with elsewhere), then eliminate those words.

15. Avoid Unnecessary *who*'s, *which*'s, and *that*'s.
Instead of saying, *A subcontractor who is working on the site must ...,* say *A subcontractor working on the site must ....* And instead of saying, *Documents that the Contractor shall have available for inspection include ...,* say *Documents the Contractor shall have available for inspection include ....*

16. Use *to be* Verbs Sparingly. The *to be* verbs include *was, is, are, were,* and *been.* Active verbs are usually clearer and more concise. Thus, instead of saying, *If Contractor is unable to ...,* say *If Contractor cannot ....*

17. Avoid Compound Prepositions. The expression *in order to,* which contains two prepositions, can be replaced with the single preposition, *to.* Similarly:

- Replace *by means of* with *by*.
- Replace *until such time as* with *until*.
- Replace *as a consequence of* with *because of*.
- Replace *in back of* with *behind*.
- Replace *in case of* with *if*.
- Replace *in a manner characteristic of* with *like*.

18. Avoid Nominalizations. A nominalization is a verb that has been converted to a noun. Another verb must then be put into the sentence to make it grammatical. The simple verb *alter* becomes *an alternation*, to which the verb *make* must now be added. Nominalizations are wordy and confusing. Go back to the pure verb form of the expression.

- Replace *have knowledge of* with *know*.
- Replace *submit a payment* with *pay*.
- Replace *make provision for* with *provide*.

19. Avoid Expletives. Grammarians call the phrases like *it is* and *there are* expletives. However, the *it* and *there* have no substantive content and are merely noise words inserted to satisfy the syntactical requirements of an English sentence. Expletives are thus wordy and obscure, not good characteristics in a drafted document. Some expletives are so much of our speech pattern that replacing them with other words would make the sentence ponderous and odd-sounding – as in replacing *it is raining* with *the rain is falling down*. Often, however, expletives can and should be eliminated, especially when they are used in connection with other drafting-style/usage violations, as in these two examples:

- Replace *it is the Seller's duty to* with *Seller shall*.
- Replace *there are four exceptions to the Seller's duty to repair* with *the Seller's duty to repair is subject to four exceptions*.

20. Write in the Active Voice. The active voice is usually shorter and more direct than the passive voice and is thus preferred in drafted documents. Replace *the goods shall be inspected by the Buyer* [8 words] with *Buyer shall inspect the goods* [5 words].

      21. Write in the Present Tense. A contract is said to be *constantly speaking* – both at the time it is drafted and whenever it is being applied. Use of past and future tense is thus generally unnecessary. Instead of saying, *if Builder's default was caused by*, say *if Builder's default is caused by*. And instead of saying, *Buyer will be entitled to*, say *Buyer is entitled to*.

      22. Avoid Long Noun Chains. Replace *the Architect-approved plumbing fixtures deviations list* with something more palatable, like *the list of deviations the Architect has approved for plumbing fixtures*.

      23. Draft Positively Rather Than Negatively. Instead of saying, *this section does not apply to deliveries made on or before June 10,* say *this section applies only to deliveries made after June 10.*

      24. Avoid Rhetorical and Transitional Words. Brief and memoranda writers often use words like *clearly* to make emphasis, *consequently* to express logical relations, and *in addition* to suggest sequence. These are all unnecessary in drafted documents.

      25. Use Numbered/Lettered Headings. All of the major divisions and subdivisions of a contract should be numbered or lettered and given a heading that describes their content. Bolding these headings will also set them apart from the text. Doing this enables the reader to quickly scan the bolded headings to find the provision he or she is looking for. Having done so, the reader can then refer with precision to this particular contract term in correspondence or litigation documents.

      Make sure the headings accurately reflect the substance of the text. If the heading is broader or narrower in scope than the text, this creates an ambiguity. And a disclaimer that the headings are not part of the contract, which one still finds in some old contracts, is simply an open admission of drafting inadequacy.

Lengthy contracts often contain a Table of Contents, consisting of the numbered/lettered headings and the page on which they may be found. These page cites should be the last thing that is proofed, because other last minute changes in the contract will often change the pagination.

26. Use Lists, Enumerations, Charts, and Bullets Freely. These visual techniques are enormously helpful in making a document readable and easy to use. They are also an excellent device for avoiding ambiguity.

Lists. A list consists of an introductory phrase, usually ending with a colon or a dash, that contains a word or phrase expressing the relationship between the elements that follow. Use either the cumulative *all of the following*, the weak disjunctive *one or more of the following*, or the strong disjunctive *no more than one of the following*. Each item in the list ends with a period.

> *To obtain an extension of time, Builder must do all of the following:*
>
> > *1. Obtain a certificate of need from the Architect.*
> >
> > *2. Complete Document 334-1.*
> >
> > *3. Post an additional default bond in the amount of $100 for each day of the requested extension.*

The items in the list can also consist of more than one sentence, if the substance is closely related, as in:

4. Notify the owner. Owner may waive this requirement in advance.

Enumerations. An enumeration consists of a single sentence, with the relationship between the items in the list being indicated by an *and* or *or* connective following the penultimate item in the series.

Seller may deliver the goods by

(1) truck,

(2) rail, or

(3) air.

It is unnecessary to put the *and* or *or* after each enumeration.

When drafting lists and enumerations, make sure all the items in the series are grammatically parallel, so that the lead phrase can be connected to any item in the series without confusion. The following enumeration does not satisfy that requirement.

Upon Buyer's default, Seller may

(1) cancel the contract,

(2) resell the goods and recover the difference in the contract price and the resale price, and

(3) Buyer agrees to pay Seller's attorneys fees in any action Seller brings under this contract.

Item (3) obviously does not tie in with the introductory phrase, either grammatically or substantively. It should be put in a separate provision.

Since an enumeration is a single sentence, another sentence cannot be inserted in the middle of it, as in this example:

> *Landlord will provide*
>
> *(1) heating and cooling,*
>
> *(2) hot and cold water. Tenant may supply a water filtration system at Tenant's own expense.*
>
> *(3) garbage removal, and*
>
> *(4) maintenance of the common areas.*

Bullets. Bullets can be used in lieu of numbered or lettered lists and are especially appropriate for documents designed for mass consumption, where it helps the reader to understand all of the critical points. For example:

> *Before signing this loan agreement, make sure –*
>
> ● *That you have read all of it.*
>
> ● *That you understand what it says.*
>
> ● *And that you have consulted with an attorney if you want to.*

Note: Personal pronouns like *I, you, we, our,* and *us* should be used only in documents where informality and easy comprehension are important, as in certain consumer contracts. They serve no purpose in a complex commercial contract and, indeed, can be a source of confusion when multiple parties are involved.

Charts. Charts are useful for expressing complex data clearly and concisely, as in the following delivery schedule:

Item	Time	Place	Mode
Hats	June	New York	Truck
Coats	July	Boston	Rail
Suits	August	Chicago	Air

27. Avoid Gender-Specific Pronouns and Terms. This is probably more of a problem for statutory drafters than contract drafters. The contracting parties are often specific, real people; they have a gender, and using gender specific pronouns when referring to them is appropriate. When one of the parties is a business entity, the proper pronoun is *it*, although repeating the proper name is probably safer.

The contract drafter may, however, encounter gender-specific pronoun problems when drafting printed form-contracts that will be used in multiple transactions – credit documents, leases, invoices, and the like. For example, how does one avoid the *If Borrower defaults, he . . . .* configuration?

Several conventions are totally unacceptable. These include *he/she*, *(s)he*, and the random alternating use of *he* and *she*. Moreover, using the plural but the gender-neutral pronoun *they* with a singular noun like *Borrower* is a perversion of standard English. Although wordy, *he or she* can be used as an option of last resort. The better alternatives include the following:

● Delete the pronoun. *Tenant may repaint the interior but before doing so he [omit] must notify Landlord.*

• Repeat the noun. *Tenant may repaint the interior but before doing so <u>Tenant</u> must notify Landlord.*

• Change the pronoun to *the, a,* or *this*. Change *exercise <u>his</u> right of first refusal* to *exercise <u>the</u> right of first refusal.*

• Reword to avoid the problem. Instead of saying, *If Buyer fails to report the discovered defect within 10 days, <u>he</u> forfeits the right of rescission,* say, *To rescind delivery, <u>Buyer</u> must report . . . .*

• As a matter of last resort, use the passive voice. Change *Tenant must file <u>his</u> notice of intention to renew within 30 days prior to . . .* to *the Tenant's notice of intention to renew must be filed within 30 days prior to . . . ."*

Another form of words that are considered gender-specific include those that end in -*man*. These can usually be avoided. *Salesman*, for example, can easily be replaced with *sales agent*.

Exercise # 3 – Drafting Style and Usage. Each of the following provisions contains one or more errors discussed in this chapter. Identify the errors and edit the provisions accordingly.

1.   If a Borrower is more than three (3) working days late in making a payment, he will be assessed a penalty of two percent (2%) of the outstanding loan amount for each additional day the payment is late.

2.   WHEREAS, Mark Twain (the Party of the First Part) and Rudyard Kipling (the Party of the Second Part) are desirous of establishing who can write the most ribald short story, the Party of the First Part and the Party of the Second Part do hereby covenant, contract, and agree to the

following terms for a contest that will determine who excels in that regard.

3.   Purchaser may select two red and/or green balls.

4.   In order to obtain a copy of the Architect's certificate of compliance, Owner must request said certificate in writing and submit a payment of $25.00 for the processing fee.

5.   Seller shall utilize the services of one of the common carriers specified in Paragraph 6 and shall commence shipments by no later than January 4, 2002. If necessitated by the exigencies of climatic circumstances, including the probabilistic expectation of any form of precipitation, Seller shall ship the grain in containers that are impervious to hydrous substances.

6.   On July 5, 2003, if it is reasonably anticipated by Contractor that the wetlands permit will not be issued by the Corps of Engineers by January 5, 2004, the Contractor shall begin site preparation on the uplands portion of the tract.

7.   First, Seller will select a brand of hydroelectric generators from what is available in the Japanese market. Next, Seller will arrange for shipment of 16 generators. On the other hand, Buyer may elect to make those arrangements directly. Finally, Seller will send three technicians

to Buyer's plant to supervise the installation of the generators. Upon delivery of the generators, Buyer will pay $258,000 by certified check. In addition, Buyer will provide suitable housing and transportation for the three technicians for a period of time not to exceed two weeks.

Chapter 4
Avoiding Ambiguities

Ambiguity is the cardinal sin of drafting. Ambiguity exists when a contract provision is subject to two or more mutually exclusive interpretations. Ambiguity is the mother of litigation. And litigation is the antithesis of good drafting.

There are three kinds of ambiguities:

- Contextual ambiguities.

- Semantic ambiguities.

- Syntactical ambiguities.

A. Contextual Ambiguity. A contextual ambiguity arises when one provision in a contract says one thing, while another provision says the contrary. A contract cannot simultaneously provide that the risk of loss does not shift until buyer accepts delivery at its factory and also make the buyer responsible for damage that occurs during transit.

Contextual ambiguities can be avoided by a technique called *cross checking*. Instead of merely reviewing the contract provision-by-provision in the order in which they are written, the drafter also needs to review it topically – looking, for example, at every provision that touches on risk of loss, regardless of where it is located within the contract. Although in a well organized contract all the provisions dealing with the same topic will usually be together, making it easy to see inconsistencies, this is not always possible. For example, in a lease agreement provisions relating to the *payment* of the security deposit may appear early in the agreement, while provisions relating to its *return* may appear at the end. Both sets of provisions dealing with the security deposit should be checked to ensure that they are totally consistent.

B. Semantic Ambiguity. A semantic ambiguity arises out of the words themselves. The drafter should always examine every word from the perspective of *the reader in bad faith*. If the drafter intends one thing but a colorable argument exists that the words mean something else, then the drafter should add some clarifying language. The words and phrases that are most likely to produce semantic ambiguity are as follows:

1. Homonyms. A homonym is a word with two or more meanings. Homonyms, such as the word *doctor*, can thus create ambiguity. Usually, this kind of ambiguity can be resolved by reference to the context of the contract. When used in connection with the qualifications for the Chief of Surgery at a hospital, the term *doctor* is not likely to be construed as referring to a Ph.D. rather than an M.D.

Context, however, will not always resolve the ambiguity. For example, the word *public* may mean a place that is generally open to the public, a place that is visible from a place generally open to the public, property owned by the government, or only government property that is generally open to the public. It may not be apparent from the context of the contract which meaning is intended.

Residence and *reside* are also of uncertain meaning. An employment contract that requires a city employee to *reside* in the city could be referring to the employee's permanent legal domicile or it could be referring merely to the employee's current dwelling place. The word is also sometimes used to indicate citizenship.

Since the word *while* is used both to express a time element and in the sense of *although*, it can be ambiguous. Suppose a contract says, *While the goods are subject to a temporary import tax, Seller may impose a 6% surcharge.* Does Seller's privilege of imposing the surcharge exist only during the time the tax is in effect? Or does it mean that despite the existence of this tax (construing it to mean *although*), Seller may also impose a surcharge?

Even a simple word like *corporation* can be ambiguous. If the contract is between the Acme Corporation and the Beta Corporation and at some point it refers to *the corporation*, which corporation does it mean? Similarly, in a famous contracts case, a reference to the ship *Peerless* was found to be ambiguous because there were two ships of that name.

2. *And.* This word can be used in either its joint or its several sense. *A and B* could thus refer to a single entity possessing the characteristics of A and B. Or it could refer to two separate entities. Does a reference to *red and white hats* refer to hats, each possessing the two colors? Or does it refer to red hats and white hats? The drafter must use additional words to clarify the intended meaning.

3. *Or.* This word can have an inclusive or an exclusive meaning. *A or B* can mean *A or B or possibly both.* Or it could mean *A or B but not both.* Although *or* is usually construed in its inclusive sense, the better practice is to make this clear by stating, for example, that the seller may supply *widgets or didgets, or both.* Conversely, if the exclusive meaning is intended, say *either widgets or didgets.*

4. *And/or.* Drafters sometimes use *and/or* as a shorthand way of saying *A or B or both.* However, not all courts have construed it that way and have, indeed, declared it to be fatally ambiguous. Thus, it should be avoided.

5. *Between...and by, from...to,* and *until.* When used in connection with dates, these terms raise questions about whether the stated date is included or not. For example, does *this option may be exercised until July 3* include July 3 or not? Literally, it does not and many courts have construed it that way, although most people would assume otherwise. The same ambiguity exist in *between July 3 and July 8* and *from July 3 to July 8.* Are July 3 and July 8 included or not? The safest course is to use *after...and before,* together or individually, rather than any of the terms listed above, as in *acceptance of this offer must be accomplished before July 4.*

6. *Over X years of age.* If the reference is to 21, does this mean the day of the person's 21st birthday? Or does it mean when the person reaches his or her 22nd birthday? One can say *21 years old or older* or *when Jane has passed her 21st birthday.*

7. *Herein.* Apart from being stylistically objectionable, terms like *herein, aforementioned,* and *hereunder* are ambiguous because it is never clear what the reference is to. Does the *herein* refer to that section or paragraph only? Or does it refer to the entire contract? The other terms are similarly flawed. Be specific. Instead of saying *herein,* say *this paragraph* or *this contract.*

C. Syntactic Ambiguity. Syntactic ambiguity emerges from the order in which words are used, their tense, and how they are punctuated. The major forms of syntactic ambiguity are as follows:

1. Ambiguity of Modification. Suppose a contract contains the following:

> *Publisher shall send promotional literature to all lawyers, accountants, and investment counselors who work for financial institutions.*

Is the publisher bound to send promotional literature to all lawyers and accountants, regardless of whether they work for financial institutions? Under the rule of the last antecedent, the *who* modifier applies only to *investment counselors.* But not all courts follow that rule of construction – hence the ambiguity. This ambiguity can be resolved by tabbing or enumerating each item in the series.

> *Publisher shall send promotional literature to all*
>
> *(a) lawyers,*

> *(b) accountants, and*
>
> *(c) investment counselors*
>
> *who work for financial institutions.*

That makes it clear that the *who* clause modifies all three categories. Or it could be clarified this way:

> *Publisher shall send promotional literature to all (a) lawyers, (b) accountants, and (c) investment counselors who work for financial institutions.*

That makes it clear that the *who* clause modifies only investment counselors.

The ambiguity is even more acute when items in a series are bracketed by both trailing and leading modifiers. Suppose a contract refers to *tax-exempt corporations and unincorporated associations providing relief to low-income families.* What do *tax-exempt* and *providing relief to low-income families* modify? Four possible interpretations exist. It could mean:

> (1)   *tax-exempt corporations*
> *and*
> *unincorporated associations providing relief. . . .*
>
> (2)   *tax-exempt*
>   *corporations*
> *and*
>   *unincorporated associations*
> *providing relief. . . .*
>
> (3)   *tax-exempt*
>   *corporations . . . .*

and
unincorporated associations providing relief . .
. .

or

(4)   tax-exempt corporations
and
unincorporated associations
providing relief. . . .

The ambiguity of the original expression can again be resolved through tabbing or enumeration, as in: *(a) tax-exempt corporations and (b) unincorporated associations providing relief to low-income families*, assuming that is what is intended.

2. Truncated Passive. As a matter of style, drafters should avoid the passive voice because it is generally wordier and more indirect than the active voice. A passive voice sentence, however, becomes ambiguous when the actor is omitted. *The bank shall be notified of any unexpected delays.* Who has the duty to notify the bank?

3. The Serial Comma. Apart from considerations of symmetry, the drafter should always use the serial comma to avoid ambiguity. The serial comma is the comma following the item just before the *and* or the *or* in the listing of a series of items. Admittedly, its omission will not create an ambiguity in most cases, particularly when *or* is the connective. But consider the following:

Seller shall deliver shirts in the following
colors: red, white, blue and green.

Does this mean that there are four classes of shirts? Or three, one containing both blue and green?

Exercise # 4 – Avoiding Ambiguity. Identify the ambiguity in each of the following. That is, be prepared to state specifically what the two or more possible meanings might be and show how each intended meaning could be more clearly expressed.

1. Causes of Termination of Benefits. Medical coverage terminates for all Dependents who are not residing in the domicile of the Insured and who are over the age of 21.

2. If the wholesale price of wheat grain in the Chicago market between July 1 and July 15 remains less than $10 per cubic ton, then Buyer will purchase no less than 500 cubic tons at the market price.

3. Disputes under this contract shall be resolved by a panel appointed by the architect consisting of three neutrals, two attorneys certified in Construction Law and one attorney certified in Environmental Law.

4. No term in this contract shall be construed as sanctioning the purchase of bolts from another source. [You may need to consult a legal dictionary to figure this one out.]

5. Following Employee's termination of employment with Acme Industrials, Employee will not work as an engineering consultant for any Montana nuclear facility, maritime construction company, or government agency that uses Safecore Widgets in the course of its operations.

6. VI. <u>Periodic Payments</u>. Owner shall pay Contractor –

(a) $10,000 upon completion of the foundation,

(b) $15,000 upon completion of the exterior framing, and

(c) the remaining $60,000 in proportion to the percentage of the remaining work that is completed each month; with the payments described herein first being approved by the architect.

7. Contractor shall install glass or brass door knobs on all interior doors.

8. [In a contract for the sale of a car]:

a. <u>Identity</u>: a 1948 Black Chevrolet coup, in operable condition.

b. <u>Price</u>: $5,000, payable upon delivery.

c. <u>Delivery</u>: Three weeks from the date of this contract, at 647 Ross Road, Wateree, South Carolina.

d. <u>Warranties</u>: Automobile is being sold **AS IS** and Seller disclaims all warranties, express or implied.

9. This section applies to 4-wheel drive SUVs and trucks manufactured after 1998.

10. After approval of the plans has been

obtained, Lending Institution shall be notified, thus beginning the running of the 180-day period referred to in paragraph 6.g.

Chapter 5
Definitions

Definitions are to a drafted document what salt is to the main dish of a dinner. They enhance palatability enormously, but must be used with discretion. Put differently, they are powerful tools that when used sloppily can cause many problems, because the courts will take them at face value and construe the contract accordingly.

A. What to Avoid.

1. Unnecessary Definitions. Do not define a term that already has an established and perfectly adequate dictionary, commercial, or legal meaning. The term *refrigerator* in a lease for a furnished apartment hardly needs to be defined. The tendency to define virtually every word that is used in a document is precisely the kind of hyper-technicality that clients find so off-putting.

However, before concluding that a definition is unnecessary, the drafter should consult both an unabridged dictionary and *Words and Phrases*. The latter provides judicial interpretations of terms that are often found in drafted documents. The drafter may discover that the dictionary definition of an ordinary word is not the same as the judicial definition or, as is often the case, that a particular term has several judicially approved meanings. In either case, a definition is necessary.

2. Humpty-Dumpty Definitions. Do not give a wildly different meaning to a term that already has an established dictionary, commercial, or legal meaning. The drafter, along with Humpty Dumpty who said words mean whatever he says they mean, has absolute linguistic liberty here. But the reader is going to be confused if you define *refrigerator* to mean *the first Thursday in June*.

3. Definitions By Reference. Do not incorporate definitions by reference to other documents, as in *"Franchisee" means the same thing it means in the Master Franchisee/Franchisor Agreement*. You cannot assume that a definition that mirrors the intent of the parties in one contract will necessarily mirror the intent of even the same parties in another contract. For example, a complex business transaction may involve several separate contracts. What the parties intended for the term *net profits* to mean in one contract is not necessarily what they intended for it to mean in a contract dealing with another aspect of the transaction.

A contractual incorporation of a set of statutory definitions is also an invitation to misunderstanding and litigation. For example, the term *disruptive speech* might be defined narrowly in a statute dealing with grounds for the termination of public employees, while this definition might not be inadequate in a private employment context, where the employer's prerogative of termination is not subject to constitutional limitations. It would be drafting error to just mindlessly adopt the statutory definition by reference, as in *"Disruptive Speech" means what it means under the South Carolina School Discipline Statute, S.C. Code § 15-478-384(A)(6)*. Moreover, what happens if the statute is later amended? Does this automatically amend the contract as well?

Even if these other definitions truly reflect the intent of the parties, restate them expressly and do not force the parties (and others using the contract) to go to some other source to determine the meaning of terms.

4. Circular Definitions. Do not define the term in reference to itself, as in *"Alcoholic beverages" means liquor, beer, wine, brandy, and other alcoholic beverages*. It is, however, permissible to define a broad term by reference to what would normally be only a subclass of that term. For example, *"Children" means children under the age of 18.*

5. One-Shot Definitions. Do not define a term that is going to be used only once in the document. This is called a *one-shot definition*. One of the several functions of definitions is to provide a shorthand label for a complex legal or factual concept, so that the description in full does not have to be repeated every time the concept is referred to later in the document. See ¶ B.2. below. No economy of words is achieved, however, by defining the term and then using it only once.

6. Definitional Mazes. Do not force the reader to work through several definitions to learn the meaning of a single word. This happens when the drafter includes within one definition a word that is further defined in another definition, which also contains terms that are themselves defined in still more definitions. The internal revenue code is infamous for this. Do not emulate the practice in your contracts.

7. Substance. Never include substantive provisions in definitions. If the parties intend for the Buyer to have a duty to accept delivery of the goods at Seller's warehouse, make that a substantive provision of the contract. Do not simply sneak it into the definition of warehouse, as in *"Warehouse," where seller shall accept delivery of the goods, means 217 Amarillo Street, Abilene, Texas.*

B. When and How to Create Definitions. The drafter should use definitions in four situations:

1. To Create a Shorthand Label. This is usually done with respect to the names of the parties and other entities referred to in the contract. These are often called *vest pocket definitions*, because they are usually not included in the definitions section. Rather, they are indicated by putting the shorthand label in parentheses – and sometimes with quotes – immediately after the name when it is used the first time.

> *G.W. Smith International Structural Steel Assembly and Erection Company, Inc. (Contractor) and Biloxy Land Development Company and Associates (Owner) mutually agree to the following terms and conditions.*

2. To Provide a Label For a New Legal or Factual Concept. Suppose that in a construction contract the owner wants to specifically indicate, by name, the persons with authority to speak on behalf of the Owner with respect to various aspects and phases of the construction process.   These individuals have no existing collective label. They are a new concept or construct. To avoid having to repeatedly list all of them by name, the drafter may create a label, like *Owner's Representatives*, and define that term by reference to the named individuals.

This is called a *stipulative definition*. As used in the contract, the term means exactly what it is defined to mean – neither more nor less. The word *means* is used to create this kind of definition.

> *"Owner's Representative" means Owner's Purchasing Agent, G.W. Harding; the Architect, Harold Halley; the Southeast Region Field Representative, Oscar Grunch; and Owner's attorney, Kathrine E. Darrow.*

3. To Expand or Define Broadly a Word With a Dictionary Meaning. A dictionary definition may be close to what the drafter has in mind, but not exactly so. And almost all words possess some degree of vagueness. A drafter, thus, may want to either expand the dictionary definition or ensure that marginal entities, which a court might or might not treat as being encompassed by the term, are in fact included.

This is called an *enlarging definition*. It takes the dictionary meaning of a word as the point of departure and adds to or clarifies the scope of its inclusion. The words *includes* or *includes but is not limited to* are used to create enlarging definitions.

> *"Compensation" includes the cash value of non-monetary bonuses, gifts, and Company product discounts.*

4. To Limit or Define Narrowly a Word With a Dictionary Meaning. Conversely, the dictionary definition of a word may be broader than the drafter desires, or the drafter may simply want to ensure a particular entity is excluded.

This is called a *limiting definition.* It takes the dictionary meaning of a word as the point of departure and constricts or clarifies the scope of its exclusion. The words *does not include* are used to create limiting definitions.

> *"Furnishings" does not include window drapes, shades, or blinds.*

Exercise # 5 – Creating Definitions

1. Assume a contract between a farmer's cooperative and individual farmers that deals exclusively with the storage and sale of wheat, corn, barley, rye, oats, rice, millet, and cotton seed. Unless you think the dictionary meaning of an existing word is already adequate, create a definition that will cover those specific items and no more.

2. Assume that you are drafting a contract that will give a publishing company the exclusive right to publish, distribute, and sell all of your client's "books," both existing and those that may be written within the next five years. Most of what your client writes are 300 to 500 pages long, are broken down into chapters, and otherwise fit into the conventional definition of a "book." You want to make sure that the contract does not also cover the 10 to 15 page tracts or pamphlets your client writes from time to time. Draft a definition to accomplish that.

3. Your client owns a fleet of delivery trucks and automobiles used by sales agents. You have drafted a proposed contract for the provision of maintenance and repair of "Company vehicles," a term that is used several times in the proposed contract. The client points

out that it also owns several battery driven carts that are used to transport personnel and miscellaneous parts and supplies within the industrial compound. The client wants to ensure that they are covered by the contract. Accomplish this with a definition.

4. What is wrong with the following definitions?

a. [In a contract for the sale of various farm animals]

"Mule" means a hybrid or cross between a horse and a donkey.

b. [In a contract to supply beverages at a reception]

"Tea" includes herbals, coffee, carbonated drinks, wine, beer, bottled water, and scotch.

c. [In a covenant not to compete, identifying the places where a staff physician, following termination from employment with a hospital, agrees not to work]

"Health Care Facility" means what it means under S.C. Code § 32-6-647 [which identifies the facilities that are subject to State Department of Health regulations].

d. [In a contract for the sale of goods]

"Site of inspection" means Seller's business at 2234 Main Street, where Seller will provide access at least two days prior to date of delivery and sufficient tools and equipment to enable buyer to broach the cartons to ascertain if the goods meet the contract requirements and, if they do not, to elect to cancel the contract or proceed

with a price reduction, to be agreed upon
by the parties.

Chapter 6
Creating Legal Consequences

The whole point of a contract is to create certain legal consequences. Although drafters disagree to some extent over this, the following words are most commonly used to create the consequence in question.

A. Duties. A contract duty is something the non-performance of which will be considered a breach. Contract duties can be created by using either *shall* or *will*. Many drafters prefer the stronger *shall*, since it is a term of command – and also because *will* is apt to be construed as simply referring to the future. Others think of contracts primarily in terms of promise, rather than command, with *will* more accurately reflecting this promissory effect. The point, however, is to adopt one convention or another and adhere to it throughout the contract.

> *Seller shall [or will] deliver the goods within 10 days from the date of this contract.*

Duties to refrain from acting are created with the words *shall not* or *will not*. Negations of, exceptions to, and qualifications upon previously created duties are expressed by saying *is not required to*.

> *Seller will deliver the goods by no later than 10 days after the date of this contract. Seller is not required to provide notice of the exact day of delivery.*

Because the term *shall* has been used and misused in so many radically different ways and *will* does not sound particularly obligatory, some drafters have abandoned both terms and use *must* and *must not* to create duties to act or refrain from acting. This, however, deprives the drafter of a useful word for creating conditions (and *must* cannot be used for both purposes). This text adheres to the *will* or *shall* convention and reserves *must* for creating conditions.

The most frequent misuse of *shall* is in what is called a *false imperative*, where the replacement of *shall* with its equivalent, *has a duty to*, would make the sentence ludicrous, as in the following examples:

> *Seller shall have the right to inspect the goods prior to delivery.* [Seller has a duty to have the right?]

> *Seller shall have the duty to arrange for shipment within 10 days.* [Seller has a duty to have a duty?]

> *Buyer's power of acceptance shall expire in 30 days.* [The power of acceptance has a duty to expire?]

> *The contract shall be subject to the laws of the State of Texas.* [The contract has a duty to be subject to these laws?]

B. Rights. A contract right is simply the corollary of a duty. If Seller has a duty to do X, then Buyer has a right that Seller do X. Whether to express X in terms of Seller's duty or Buyer's right is a matter of drafter judgment, although the duty approach is most often used in contracts. It would be obtuse to express the payment term by reference to the seller's right to receive it rather than the buyer's duty to pay it. However, something like a landlord's entry into an apartment for repairs or to show it to prospective new tenants is best expressed in terms of a right. Rights should be created by using the words *is entitled to*.

> *If Buyer is late in making payments on three consecutive shipments, Seller is entitled to impose a surcharge of 5% on the amount due for the fourth and all subsequent shipments.*

The negation of or limitations upon existing rights can be accomplished by saying, *is not entitled to.*

> *Employee is entitled to speak publically about any matters, without fear of recrimination from the Company, but Employee is not entitled to and will not publically disparage the Company, its practices, its policies, or its products.* [Both denying the right and making it a duty not to.]

C. Privileges. A privilege differs from a right only in the sense that it does not have a direct duty-corollary. The corollary, rather, is a *no-right.* To say that Seller has a *privilege* of doing X, means that Buyer does not have a *right* that Seller do or not do X. The word *may* is used to create privileges.

Contract privileges come principally in two forms, each creating a slightly different legal consequence. The first gives the privilege-holder an option to choose between several alternatives, as in selecting how the duty of delivery will be satisfied.

> *Seller may deliver by truck, rail, or air.*

Buyer is bound to accept the goods in the manner chosen by Seller – which is to say that the Buyer has no right to reject the goods if they are delivered in any of the ways listed.

Another form of privilege gives the privilege holder the power to unilaterally create legal consequences.

> *Seller may terminate this contract on 10 days notice to Buyer.*

If the privilege is exercised, the contract is terminated and Buyer has no further rights.

D. Conditions. Conditions differ from duties in the sense that the failure of a pure condition does not constitute a breach of the contract; it merely means that certain other legal consequences will or will not attach. Conditions (satisfaction or non-satisfaction) often trigger contract rights and duties. The seller's duty to deliver may be conditioned on the buyer first doing something (condition precedent), or the seller's duty to deliver may be discharged by the buyer's failure to do something (condition subsequent).

A condition may consist of conduct or non-conduct by one of the contracting parties. In this case, the term *must* should be used.

> *To revoke acceptance, Buyer must do the following:*

When the condition relates to an external event, several words may be used, depending on the circumstances. The most common terms are *if*, *when*, and *after*. For example:

> *If a septic tank permit is not granted, Buyer is entitled to a price reduction in the amount of . . . .*

> *When an embargo is in effect, Seller's duties are suspended.*

> *After the expiration of 10 days, Buyer is entitled to a 10% reduction in the sales price.*

Since the courts are reluctant to construe a contract provision as imposing a true condition (because it requires complete and not merely substantial performance), cautious drafters sometimes expressly label a condition as such.

> *The insured must notify the company of all claims within 5 days of the injury. This notification is a condition precedent of the*

company's duty to pay and strict compliance is required.

Sometimes, a contract provision is intended to function as both a promise to perform and as a condition of the other party's return promise. Usually, the provision is worded solely in terms of promise, and the courts infer the conditional aspect. This is called a *constructive condition*. Satisfaction of the conditional aspect, however, requires only substantial performance. If the drafter intends for the provision to be both a promise and a true condition, then this must be made express.

> *Contractor will install Reading pipe in the structure* [a promise, the breach of which makes the seller liable for damages], *and if Contractor installs any other brand of pipe and refuses to replace it, Owner may cancel the contract and is not liable to Contractor for any of the work previously done, either under a contract or a quantum meruit theory of recovery* [also making installation of Reading pipe an express condition of Owner's payment duties].

E. Warranties. Most contract promises impose an obligation to do or to refrain from doing certain things. Another kind of promise relates to the quality of the goods or the existence of a certain state of affairs. This kind of promise is called a *warranty* or a *guarantee* and those are the words that drafters use to create them.

> *Seller warrants that the air conditioner is in working condition.*
>
> *Seller guarantees the seeds to be weed free.*

F. Other Legal Consequences. A miscellaneous collection of legal consequences are created by using *is*, *is not*, or some other verb.

> *Buyer's option to renew expires at 10:00 p.m. on October 23, 2005.* [Not *shall expire*, which is a false imperative.]

> *The interpretation and enforcement of this contract is governed by the laws of Texas.* [Not *shall be governed*, which is another false imperative.]

Exercise # 6 – Creating Legal Consequences

1.   Create a contractual obligation for Seller to deliver the goods to 345 Sunset Drive, Gotham City, State of Erehwon.

2.   Create a contractual entitlement on behalf of Buyer to inspect the goods at Seller's facility, 649 Sunrise Blvd., Gotham City, State of Erehwon.

3. In a contract that has imposed a duty on Buyer to pay upon delivery, now draft a provision that allows Buyer to pay in cash, with a credit card, or by certified check.

4. In a contract for the sale of wheat, draft a provision that doubles the quantity Buyer is obligated to buy if the Chicago market price on a particular date is a certain amount per ton or less.

5. In a contract for the sale of wheat, draft a provision that cancels the contract if the Chicago market price on a particular date is a certain amount per ton or more.

6. Make the provision for cancellation described in paragraph 5 above at Buyer's option, with the requirement that Buyer notify

Seller of its decision to cancel the contract within 12 hours of the announcement of the Chicago market price.

7. In a contract for the sale of your 1996 Ford Explorer, provide positive assurance to the buyer you were the vehicle's original owner.

8. In a contract between a State of South Erehwon Buyer and a State of North Erehwon Seller, make sure that South Erehwon law and rules of construction will control enforcement and interpretation of the contract.

Chapter 7
The Rules of Contract Interpretation

Most of the so-called *rules* of contract interpretation are not really rules at all. They are more like *guiding principles* that the courts adhere to with varying degrees of consistency and are often referred to as the *canons* of interpretation. Almost every rule has an exception or offsetting rule, with the plaintiff relying on one rule and the defendant on another. Ideally, a contract should be drafted so that a court does not have to resort to these problematic rules of interpretation.

The leading rules, and their implications for the drafter, are as follows:

A. The Plain Meaning or Four Corners Rule. Under the traditional version of this rule, a court will give the words of a contract, as contained within its four corners, their plain meaning. Extrinsic evidence of what the parties subjectively intended the words to mean is admissible only if the words have no plain meaning, because they are either ambiguous or excessively vague.

This rule places an enormous – but justified – burden on the drafter. The drafter should not be like Alice in Wonderland, who was a little loose with her terminology.

> *"Then you should say what you mean," the March Hare went on.*

> *"I do," Alice hastily replied; "at least – at least I mean what I say – that's the same thing, you know."*

> *"Not the same thing a bit!" said the Hatter. "Why you might just as well say that 'I see what I eat' is the same thing as 'I eat what I see.'"*

The *plain meaning rule* reflects a philosophy of individual autonomy and responsibility – that it is the duty of courts to enforce contracts, not write them. Critics, however, have pointed out that words are slippery things and that many words in the English language have no single or plain meaning. The answer to that, of course, is that the drafter should use as many words as necessary to make the meaning clear. Although modern courts are not as inclined to follow this rule as were courts in the early Twentieth Century, one never knows when a court will invoke the rule. Drafters should draft with that possibility in mind. Thus, if contract is drafted in anticipation of an application of the plain meaning rule, the drafter must make sure that this plain meaning is truly consistent with the intent of the client. Do not put yourself in the position of having to convince a judge that *Yes, literally that is what the contract says, but* . . . . and then attempt to prevail under the next rule of interpretation.

B.   The Intent of the Parties Controls. Many courts, rejecting the narrow constraints of the plain meaning rule, hold that the intent of the parties always controls and that this intent can be evidenced not only by the literal words they use, but also by extrinsic evidence and a common-sense reading of the document. For example, courts will sometimes focus on the purpose of the contract – the good to be achieved or the harm to be avoided – and construe specific contract language according to what the court thinks the parties probably would have intended if they had thought about it, even though it might not be encompassed by the plain meaning of the language.

The good drafter, however, will not force the courts to rely on this fictional, after-the-fact type of intent but will, rather, word the contract in such a way that the intent of the parties and the meaning of the contract cannot be in dispute.

C. Construe the Document as a Whole. All this means is that a court will not interpret a specific provision of the contract in isolation. If an argued-for interpretation of one provision makes it inconsistent with the broader implications of the contract, that interpretation is unlikely to prevail. Similarly, the courts are unlikely to accept an interpretation of one provision that would render another provision either redundant or superfluous.

　　　　This is why the drafter must do an across-the-board review of the document once it is drafted, to ensure that no provision is even implicitly inconsistent with another and that everything can be viewed as a coherent whole.

　　　　D. The Rule of *noscitur a sociis*. Drafters like to refer to some of these rules by their Latin names, which probably impresses no one but their mothers. In any event, this rule requires a court to construe a word, phrase, or specific provision within its context. The term *reasonable precautions to avoid damage to persons or property* could mean one thing in the context of a gunpowder manufacturing plant (where explosion is the danger), but quite another in a machine shop (where misuse or abuse of the equipment is the danger). Smoking, thus, would probably be covered in the first context, but not the second.

　　　　The competent drafter should not leave this to judicial implication. The vague and abstract *damage to persons or property* should be replaced with more precise and concrete terms.

　　　　E. The Rule of *expressio unius est exclusio alterius*. This means *the expression of one thing is the negation of others*. This is also sometimes referred to as a negative pregnant. Thus, if a contract states that the Seller *may ship by rail or truck*, this is an implied denial of permission to ship by air.

　　　　Drafters who make lists of things must take care to include everything on the list that is intended to be covered, because the courts may be unwilling to add additional items by implication. Drafters sometimes try to get around the *expressio unius* rule by adding to the list a catch-all expression like *or similar products*. This, however, leads to another problem, one the next rule is designed to remedy.

　　　　F. The Rule of *ejusdem generis*. This means *of the same kind*. Under this rule, general terms like *or similar products* would be construed as including only other products of the type or kind of those listed. The technique for applying this rule is to identify the common denominator of the listed items and then limit the general phrase to other items sharing that characteristic. The problem is that the items in the series may have several different common denominators.

Suppose, for example, that the Student Bar Association sells school supplies to law students and has an exclusive dealing arrangement with Acme Office Supplies under which Acme has the right to supply all the *notebooks, yellow pads, Bluebooks, printer paper, pens, pencils, and other similar materials* that the store sells. Can the store purchase backpacks from a different supplier? One common denominator of the listed items is that they all involve writing – either the instruments of writing or what is written upon. A backpack is not similar in that regard. On the other hand, if the common denominator is more broadly construed to be things that law students frequently use in connection with their studies, then a backpack is similar.

The point is that the drafter should not delegate to the courts the authority to make that determination on behalf of the client. Find out what the client intends and express it clearly and unequivocally.

G. The Rule Favoring Validity. If one party attempts to construe a term in a way that will make the provision or the entire contract invalid, and the other party points this out and argues for a different construction, the court will almost always adopt the construction that favors validity. For example, if a covenant not to compete could be construed as covering the entire United States and thus invalid under the common law rule of *reasonableness*, then the court would be inclined to give the provision a narrower, more reasonable interpretation.

The drafter, however, should not draft a provision that is even capable of being construed in a manner that would make that provision or the entire contract invalid, and then hope to save the document from that fate by relying on this canon of interpretation. Draft the provision so that it is valid, and clearly so.

H. The Rule Favoring the Specific Over the General. If a construction contract contains a provision that apparently applies to the quality of all materials that are used on the project, but a specific provision requires a higher or allows a lesser quality on a particular material, then the more specific provision will prevail.

The drafter, thus, needs to be aware of the relationship between various provisions, by cross-checking the document and making this specific exception to the general rule very clear, rather than relying on this rule of interpretation.

I. The Rule That Handwritten Terms Prevail Over Typed or Printed Words. Drafters often prepare form documents, which are printed and used in multiple transactions. The specific details of each transaction are written in later. Or, at the last moment, the parties may decide to add some handwritten provisions to a typed document. The danger is that what is handwritten will be expressly or implicitly inconsistent with the printed or typed version. When that happens, the courts often rely on this rule of interpretation to resolve the conflict.

The cautious drafter should thus warn the client not to make any last-minute handwritten changes or additions without checking first with counsel. And if the drafter is present when the changes are made, special care should be taken to ensure internal consistency.

J. The Rule of Construing a Document Against the Drafter. Despite the drafter's best efforts, ambiguity and fatal vagueness do sometimes creep into contracts. The drafter's client in good faith insists on one meaning, the other party to the contract insists on another.

Under this rule, the drafter's client is apt to lose. This should operate as a deterrent to drafters who are willing to draft at the margin and gamble that they will prevail if the matter is ever litigated. The deck is stacked against them.

If the specific terms of a contract document have been extensively negotiatcd, with each party contributing to the language, the contract could contain a provision stating that the contract has been *mutually drafted*, thus avoiding the application of this rule.

K. The Rule in Favor of Construing a Contract in a Way That is Consistent With Public Policy. As the philosophy of contract interpretation and enforcement has shifted away from an emphasis on individual autonomy and responsibility to one of increased social control over the terms and process of contracting, this rule has become increasingly important to the drafter. For example, an employment contract may expressly allow an employer to terminate an employee who reports the employer to a regulatory agency for alleged violations of some environmental, occupational safety, or other statute. Even if this termination is not a violation of the statute itself, a court may refuse to allow it on the grounds that it violates public policy.

The drafter must be aware of these *public policy* limitations and not draft contracts in a way that might be construed as a violation of the policy in question.

Exercise # 7 – Rules of Interpretation

Notice how all of these provisions contain drafting errors that have created potentially conflicting meanings, which must be resolved with the rules of interpretation. Identify the error and the relevant rule or competing rule.

1. Assume the following provisions in a contract:

. . . .

c. *Buyer shall purchase 10 Widgets a month at $7.00 per Widget.*

. . . .

   s. Total monthly payment per Widget: Seven dollars and fifty cents.

   The underlined portion in script is handwritten. If there are no other provisions that might affect the total price, how much does Buyer owe each month?

   2. Suppose an insurance contract covers "automobiles, trucks, buses, and similar vehicles." What argument would an insured make to establish that a dune buggy is covered? Identify characteristics of the listed items that are similar to the characteristics of a dune buggy. What argument would the insurance company make that it is not covered? Identify the characteristics of a dune buggy that it does not share with the listed items.

   3. Suppose that a contract provides that one of the parties may designate her "attorney, tax accountant, or real estate broker" to act on her behalf in a certain matter. What rule of interpretation would probably prevent her from giving her banker this authority?

   4. Suppose a contract's introductory section contains a provision stating that "all payments under this contract must be by certified check." The contract later, in several different places, specifically deals with the payments that are due for the various goods and services covered by the contract. Suppose that one of them says, "With respect to service calls, Purchaser may pay the Service Technician by personal check." A Service Technician later refuses to accept a personal check, claiming that the contract requires all payments to be by certified check. Who will prevail?

   5. An employment contract between the State Department of Health and its employees requires each employee to be "a legal resident of the United States." The Department has recently terminated Gonzales Garcia, who is a citizen of Mexico but has lived in the State most of his life. The Department maintains that the provision refers to citizenship and some extrinsic evidence of intent exists that supports that view. Garcia maintains that the provision

must refer to where one lives permanently, since a similar contract provision in another state had been found to be illegal. Who will prevail?

6. A contract requires the Seller to sell the Buyer to buy all of the "automobiles" that Buyer needs during the next three years for its sale staff, at 3% over cost. At the time, Seller was a Ford dealer and there is uncontroverted evidence that the parties intended for the contract to cover only Ford automobiles. Later, Seller also became a dealer for Toyotas. When Seller tried to supply Buyer with a Toyota, Buyer refused to accept it. Seller, however, maintains that since a Toyota is an "automobile," he is within his rights. Who will prevail?

Chapter 8
The Anatomy of a Contract Transaction

From the perspective of both the buyer and the seller, the purchase and sale of residential property may involve the most significant financial investment of their lives. This chapter will explain how the transaction is most commonly handled, without any significant direct lawyer assistance – a situation fraught with dangers to both parties. But it will also show that the situation could be even worse when an incompetent lawyer attempts to draft the contract. Finally, the chapter will demonstrate how a lawyer using the drafting processes and terminology discussed earlier in this book can produce a contract that would be at least moderately adequate and that would facilitate the completion of the transaction efficiently, effectively, and without too much rancor or frustration on anyone's part.

Caveat: The law and customs for drafting contracts for the sale of residential property vary from state to state. It is an enormously complex area of the law. The object of the chapter is not to teach you the law of real estate transactions (and my property law colleagues have enjoined me from even attempting to do that), nor is the purpose to produce a *model* or totally comprehensive contract suitable for use in all jurisdictions and situations. The focus is on the drafting process.

But, let's start at the beginning.

Most contracts for the sale of residential housing consist of a printed form prepared by a various real estate companies and trade associations (or their counsel). This form contract is similar to a coral reef in several respects – beauty *not* being one of them, however. The standard contract is intricate and detailed beyond belief. It has a highly irregular structure or organization. Parts of it are very old, consisting of provisions that obtained judicial approval in the distant past, the wording of which has not changed since. It has layer upon layer of incrustations, provisions added haphazardly over the years as omissions in the old form were discovered and new provisions became necessary because of changes in the law. And, like a narrow coral reef, all of this is packed into the two sides of a

8½ x 11piece of paper in type so small as to be almost impossible to read without magnification. Lined blank spaces, perhaps 3/16ths of an inch high and rarely long enough, are provided for the critical details of each individual transaction. The margins are narrow. The form is as potentially dangerous to buyers and sellers as coral reefs are to mariners.

The form, which typically favors the seller, is completed on behalf of the would-be buyer by a real estate agent. Primarily, this consists of filling in the blanks. Sometimes, large blocks of the printed text are also *x*'ed out because they are allegedly not applicable to that particular sale. And additional terms are often written in, using the narrow margins for that purpose. Many real estate agents are extremely competent, conscientious, and well-trained in handling routine transactions. But some are not. And almost none have the training and experience of a lawyer specializing in real estate law – who may be the only one able to see that a transaction is not as *routine* as it might appear to be.

In any event, the completed form is then submitted to the seller. It constitutes the buyer's offer. This offer is rarely accepted by the seller without change. The price has been kept intentionally low, it will often contain a long list of cosmetic repairs that the buyer would like to have done, and it sometimes even includes the sale of items that are not technically part of the realty. The seller will then make a counteroffer, substantially increasing the price, pruning the list of repairs, and deleting the items that the seller is unwilling to part with.

This counteroffer is accomplished by lining-out the unacceptable handwritten portions of the original offer and inserting the seller's own handwritten revisions, together with seller's initials. The resulting jumble of handwritten cross-outs and additions makes identifying the substance of the changes somewhat difficult.

This counteroffer is submitted to the buyer. If things go according to plan, the buyer will then submit a counter-counteroffer, in which the price is roughly half way between the buyer's original offer and the seller's counteroffer. This is done by lining out the seller's figure and inserting a new figure, with initials. If the seller agrees to this final price and initials the latest change, that ends the *drafting* process. The document is then given to the closing attorney, usually chosen by the buyer, whose paralegals and administrative assistants often do the title search and prepare all the necessary mortgage papers, disclosure statements, deeds, and other innumerable forms required by state and federal law. The attorney's signature appears on various documents, but often this is the limit of his or her direct involvement – for some do not even appear at the closing itself.

Amazingly, many of these transactions go through without a hitch, simply because they are so routine. But many do not. Sometimes, particularly if a competent attorney is finally present at the closing and explains the terms of the contract, one of the parties may object and claim that this is not what was agreed to. Or the misunderstanding may emerge after the closing, at the performance stage of the transaction. And even if the transaction is completed, the buyer's interests may not have been vigorously pressed – nor, sometimes, those of the seller either.

Occasionally that entire process is circumvented. This most often occurs when a home is for sale *By Owner*. Real estate agents, with their printed forms, are simply not involved. Often, the owner will want to have a contract available for willing buyers to sign. Or a potential buyer, seeing the *By Owner* sign, will make the initial offer in the form of a proposed contract. Rarely do owners or would-be buyers attempt to write these contracts themselves. Rather, they retain a lawyer to do it.

Indeed, it seems that this is often the first real contract a beginning lawyer is asked to draft. A friend, neighbor, relative, or college chum who intends to buy or sell a home without the services of a real estate agent will ask the neophyte to do this, perhaps in the mistaken believe that it is so simple that even the recent graduate can accomplish it without difficulty. (Drafting the equally non-existent *simple will* is also a frequent first drafting effort for young lawyers.)

In any event, let us assume that attorney Bonnie Parker has been asked by her old friend Elizabeth Borden-Loeb to draft a contract on a *For Sale By Owner* home that Elizabeth and her husband want to sell. She inherited the home from her parents, but under state marital rights law he owns a half-interest. The property includes a backyard shed sitting on skids (so that it could be moved), a detached garage, some extremely heavy and truly tacky concrete yard ornaments that merely sit on the ground and are not cemented in, an above-the-ground swimming pool that apparently leaks, and a rusted old boat trailer without wheels and a huge pile of rotting lumber and brick rubble that is piled behind the garage. The windows are covered with expensive (but of a standard size) wooden levered shades. There are stains in the ceiling in the kitchen and some dampness that clearly indicates an existing leak in the roof. From the outside, the Boxers can see that the roofing shingles are very old and will need to be replaced (which also probably accounts for the leak) and the roof sags over the great room. Some of the window sills appear to be rotten. Also, the picture window in the living room has a major crack in one corner. The Borden-Loebs want $180,000.00 for the property.

Parker, who specializes in criminal defense work, locates a *sample real estate contract* on line and digs up the printed contract form her agent used when she recently purchased her condominium (a transaction the terms of which are materially different from the sale of land and a stand-alone structure). From these sources, she cobbles together the following contract:

CONTRACT FOR THE SALE AND CONVEYANCE OF REAL PROPERTY

Elizabeth Borden-Loeb and Richard Loeb (hereinafter referred to as the "Party of the First Part) do hereby agree, covenant, and contract to sell the

property hereinafter described to _____
*(hereinafter referred to as the "Party of the Second
Party").*

666 Bates Road, Fall River, Massachusetts.

*Eighteen Thousand dollars and no cents
($180,000), of which Five Hundred dollars and no
cents ($500) has been paid in hand to Party of the First
Part to be held in escrow as earnest money and applied
to the total purchase price or forfeited by the Party of
the Second Part in the event the sale does not go thru.*

*The owner of this property shall sell this property
subject to all existing encumbrances.*

*If a new loan is obtained, purchaser must bear
the closing cost expenses and all loan application fees.
Purchaser must also have CASH, CASHIER'S CHECK,
or CERTIFIED FUNDS at closing. Purchaser agrees
to apply for financing within five (5) days of the date of
this contract.*

*The home is not covered by any seller warranties
regarding structural soundness, condition of the roof,
appliances, plumbing, or electrical systems.*

*Party of the First Part agrees to convey by
marketable title and to have prepared a proper
statutory warranty deed.*

Closing date is _____.

_____   _____
Elizabeth Borden-Loeb

_____   _____
Richard Loeb

PARTIES OF THE   *PARTIES OF THE*
FIRST PART   *SECOND PART*

                    ADDENDUM

____ *(Seller's Initials)*   ____*(Buyer's Initials)*

Parker explains that if the parties think of anything else they want included in the contract, they can simply write it in under the *Addendum* and initial it. Elizabeth and Richard are pleased with Parker's handiwork and she runs off several copies for them. They post a *For Sale By Owner* sign in the front yard.

A few days later, Gus and Samantha Boxer see the sign, go through the house, and decide it is exactly what they want – although perhaps not at that price, and they are concerned over some of the obvious defects. Richard Loeb says they can sign a contract right then, they'll fix everything, and produces a copy of the Parker contract. The Boxers review it and say, wisely, that they want to check with their lawyer first. The next day, they bring it to you.

You are appalled. You note the following stylistic defects.

There are no numbered headings.

line 1 – *sale and conveyance* is wordy and redundant.

lines 5 & 8 – the *hereinafter* and *Party of . . . .* language is archaic legalese. In addition, in line 9 it becomes *Party of the Second Party*, which is a glaring demonstration of sloppy drafting.

The better practice is to simply identify the Borden-Loebs as *(Seller)* and the Boxers as *(Buyer)*.

lines 20, 23, 25 & 26 – note too that after establishing a *shorthand* designation for the parties, the contract fails to adhere rigorously to it, later using terms like *owner, purchaser, seller,* and *Part<u>ies</u> of the* [various] *Part*[s].

line 6 – *hereby* is legalese.

line 6 – *agree, covenant, and contract* is a redundant triplet.

line 7 – *hereinafter* is legalese.

line 11 – presumably, this is the *property hereinafter described.* But what if the contract also contains other property addresses? This should be specifically identified as the property that is being sold.

lines 13-14 – these lines contain a textual ambiguity of the first order! The written out dollar amount and the parenthetical dollar amount are not the same. People tend not to read written out dollar amounts. Both parties will thus assume that the numerical version is accurate. But under the canons of interpretation, a written out dollar amount usually prevails over a numerical version. If Parker's clients sign this monstrosity, they may end up selling their property for $18,000! A court might construe the contract to reflect the probable intent of the parties, but Parker faces some potential malpractice liability here.

lines 13-15 – indeed, spelling out and putting the figure in numerical form is a senseless and dangerous redundancy. Use only the numerical figure; just make sure you have the commas, the periods, and the zeros right!

line 15 – *paid in hand* is archaic legalese.

line 18 – *in the event* is a wordy way to say *if*.

line 18 – do not use unconventional, colloquial spelling – replace *thru* with *through*.

lines 20-21 – it is odd indeed to create a duty (using *shall*) requiring the seller to sell subject to all existing encumbrances. Since the document is creating that legal consequence directly, the operative words are: *the property is being sold subject to all existing encumbrances* – and then list and limit them to *deed restrictions, existing easements and rights-of-way, and existing statutes and zoning ordinances*.

lines 23 & 25 – the word *must* merely creates a condition, something the buyer has to do for some other consequence to attach. Paying the closing cost expenses and loan application fees should be expressed in terms of a duty, using *will* or *shall* – so that if the buyer refuses to do so and the deal falls through, this will be a breach of the contract, enabling the seller to recover damages. The same is true with respect to the method of payment.

lines 25-26 – this CAPITALIZATION is totally unnecessary here.

line 26 – the *agrees* suggests that this was intended to create a duty, but the correct word for doing this is *will* or *shall*.

line 27 – *five (5)* is redundant numeration.

lines 52-59 – giving the parties the license to draft other additional provisions to the contract is not only a cart blanc invitation to other stylistic horrors, it is also a ready source of substantive errors, omissions, and ambiguities. If the client writes in something that inures to the client's enormous disadvantage later on, the attorney would undoubtedly have malpractice liability.

You keep these stylistic (and quasi-substantive) objections to yourself. Of more concern are the substantive defects, which you share with the Boxers, as follows.

First, the seller is not the proper person to hold the escrow money. If the deal falls through under circumstances requiring its return to the buyer and the seller refuses to return it, a lawsuit may be necessary. It is usually held by the buyer's closing attorney. Then, if a condition fails through no fault of the buyer or the seller simply breaches, the attorney can return the money to the client. On the other hand, if the client breaches and forfeits the earnest money, then the attorney will be under a legal and ethical duty to pay it to the seller. A lawsuit to collect it is rarely necessary.

Second, no mortgage company will lend money on a home that does not have termite and HVAC (heating, ventilation, air conditioning) letters – that is, certifications that the property is free of current termite infestation, damage from prior infestations, and water damage and that the heating and cooling units work. The contract (which the mortgage company will review when making the loan decision) must have a provision dealing with this. Obtaining these letters is usually at the seller's cost.

Form contracts often make obtaining the necessary letters a mere condition of the seller's duty to sell. Thus, if the termite inspector or the heating/cooling company finds problems and cannot issue a certification letter, and the seller does not want to make the necessary repairs, all this means is that a condition fails and the sale is off. Thus, some buyer-drafted contracts make this a duty, and a seller who signs the contract without realizing this will discover later that they have assumed a duty to make the necessary repairs, regardless of the expense. This is but another example of how a buyer's and a seller's interests may diverge over the specific content of a common contract term – with one version favoring the seller and the other the buyer. The Boxers want to make this a contractual duty.

Third, you know the Boxers own their present home, subject to a heavy mortgage. You ask if they can make the down payment on the new home (the difference between the sale price and the amount the bank will loan) or carry two mortgage payments for a while. They reply that they could do neither and had *assumed* that the actual purchase of the new house could be delayed until they were able to sell their old house. You advise them that their assumption was incorrect. They would have been required to close on the date given, regardless of the sale of their old house. You suggest, however, that you can take care of the situation. You explain that it would be a rare seller indeed who would be willing to postpone the transaction indefinitely, pending the sale of another property. The usual practice, rather, is to give the buyer an option. The seller can keep the property on the market even after the contract is signed. If a better offer comes in, then the Boxers would have the option of waiving the contingency (prior sale of their house) and going ahead with the transaction (which means they must find some additional short-term financing for the down payment and for several monthly payments) or terminating it and having their earnest money returned. They are not real happy over that, but agree to proceed on that basis.

You ask if they saw any obvious defects in the house. They tell you what they saw, as indicated above, but that they had the oral assurances of the seller that all of this would be repaired. You suggest they need more than that. You ask about window coverings. Samantha Boxer says the house has wooden Venetian blinds that she expects will come with the house. You suggest this needs to be expressly included in the contract. You inquire if there is anything on the property that they want removed as a part of the sale. They mention the concrete yard art, the above-the-ground pool, the boat trailer, and the trash – but again express surprise that you would ask, since they assumed this sort of thing always had to be removed. You suggest that this is not necessarily so. You ask if there is anything else on the property that they assume is included in the sale, and they mention the shed on sleds. You suggest it might not be included in the current contract.

With respect to the existing defects and the items the Boxers want removed, you suggest that the contract should impose a duty on the seller's part to remove or fix these things to the buyer's satisfaction. But you further you conclude that the Boxers should also insist on having the property inspected by a Certified Residential Property Building Inspector and that the sale be conditioned on the buyer's satisfaction with the report – or the seller's correction of anything found to be unsatisfactory to the buyers. Unlike the repair of clearly existing structural defects, which is typically made a duty, this additional satisfaction with the state of the property is usually made only a condition of the sale. Inspectors vary enormously in what they consider a problem and buyer satisfaction is an highly subjective determination (usually limited only by good faith) that varies from buyer to buyer. Thus, rather than correcting alleged defects found and objected to by one inspector/buyer combination, the seller may hope that other inspectors/buyers would not be so persnickety and elect to let the contract fail for non-satisfaction of the condition. The Boxers seem satisfied with this and are reassured that you are looking out for their interests.

There are some other provisions that you will want to put into the contract, but you can explain them to the Boxers later. Thus, on the basis of the information that you have, you draft the following:

CONTRACT FOR THE
SALE AND PURCHASE
OF RESIDENTIAL PROPERTY

Elizabeth Borden-Loeb and Richard Leob ("Seller"), who are joint owners of the Property located located at 666 Bates Road, Fall River, Massachusetts ("Property") agree to sell, and Gustavus Boxer and Samantha Boxer ("Buyer") agree to purchase the Property, subject to the following terms and conditions.

A. *What the Sale Includes*

Seller will convey title or ownership rights to the real property, the house, the garage, the storage shed, the Venetian blind window coverings, and any fixtures except the above-ground swimming pool.

B. *Removal of Non-Sale Items*

Seller will remove from the property the above ground swimming pool, the cement yard ornaments, the boat trailer behind the garage, and the lumber and brick rubble behind the garage.

C. *Correction of Defects*

1. Seller will, to Buyer's satisfaction –

> *a. replace the picture window in the living room;*
>
> *b. repair the sag in the roof over the great room;*
>
> *c. install new roofing shingles on the entire roof and warrant that the leak in the kitchen has been fixed; and*
>
> *d. replace all rotten window sills.*

2. Seller, at Seller's expense, will obtain letters, and supply them to the closing attorney at least five days prior to closing, certifying –

a. that the structures subject to the sale are free of current termite or other insect infestation, that there is no damage resulting from prior infestations, and that there is no water damage; and

b. that the heating and air conditioning units are functional.

3. Seller will make whatever repairs or replace whatever equipment as is necessary to obtain the certification letters.

4. In addition, Buyer may, at Buyer's expense, have the property inspected by a Certified Residential Property Building Inspector. This inspection and report must be accomplished no later than two weeks before the closing date. If, for any reason, Buyer is not satisfied with the Inspector's report and Seller elects not to make the necessary repairs, Buyer may rescind this contract and obtain from the closing attorney a return of the earnest money.

D. Destruction or Damage to the Property

1. If, between the execution of this contract and the closing date, the property or any of the structures or items located on it that are subject to this sale are destroyed or damaged by fire or other causes, Buyer may rescind the contract and obtain a return of earnest money.

2. Seller will otherwise maintain the property, structures, and yard in the same condition as they are on the date of the execution of this contract, subject to normal wear and tear.

E. Inspection of Property

On the day prior to closing, Buyer may inspect the property to determine if Seller's duties to repair, replace, and maintain, as set forth above, have been met. Seller's failure to repair, replace, and maintain is a material breach, and Buyer may both rescind the contract and obtain damages for breach.

F. Title and Deed

1. Seller will deliver, free of all encumbrances (including mortgages and liens), a fee simple, general warranty deed, with revenue stamps attached, made out to Gustavus Boxer and Samantha Boxer.

2. This sale is subject to a determination by the closing attorney that Seller can convey a fee simple title, not encumbered by any outstanding mortgages, liens, or claims. If the closing attorney is not satisfied with title and cannot obtain title insurance on the property, Buyer may rescind the contract and obtain a return of the earnest money.

3. This sale and the title to the Property are subject to all existing easements and restrictive covenants and to all governmental statutes, ordinances, rules, and regulations. If, between the execution of this contract and closing the Property is condemned or changes in existing law make it unusable as residential property, then Buyer may rescind the contract and obtain a return of the earnest money.

G. Price

1. Buyer will pay $140,000 for the Property.

2. Upon the execution of this contract, Buyer will pay to Samuel A. Meddling, who will be the closing attorney, $1,400 as earnest money. Closing attorney is authorized –

> *a. to pay this to Seller at closing of if Buyer breaches, or*

> *b. return the money to Buyer if a contingency fails or Seller breaches.*

3. At closing, Buyer will pay the remaining amount to the closing attorney who will pay this amount, together with the funds received from the mortgage company, first to any existing mortgage or lien holders of the Property (in return for acknowledgment of the satisfaction of the mortgage or lien), in satisfaction of other closing expenses of Seller, and then to Seller.

H. Financing

Upon the execution of this contract, Buyer will make a reasonable effort to obtain financing to pay the agreed upon purchase price (above whatever Buyer pays for in cash). If Buyer is unable to obtain the necessary financing at under 8% interest and with no more than 2 points, then Buyer may rescind the contract and obtain a return of the earnest money.

I. Sale Contingent on Buyer's Sale of Current Residence

> *1. This sale is contingent on the prior sale (closing and receipt of purchase price) of Buyer's current residence, 28 Shady Lane, Lesser Falls, Massachusetts.*

> *2.   Pending the satisfaction of this contingency, if Seller obtains an equal or better offer to buy, Seller must inform Buyer of this in writing. Buyer then has three days in which to either waive the contingency and proceed with the transaction or rescind the contract and obtain a return of earnest money.*

J. Closing

> *1. Closing is at 10 a.m. on October 23, 2003, at the office of the closing attorney, 647 Barrister Way, Boston, Massachusetts.*

> *2.   If any contingency has not been satisfied as of the closing date indicated above, the closing is automatically*

extended two weeks. This is a one-time extension, unless the parties expressly agree otherwise.

K. Miscellaneous Provisions

1. [a choice of law provision, indicating that Massachusetts contract and property law controls.][1]

2. [a merger clause, declaring this to be the final and exclusive agreement between the parties.][2]

3. [a no-oral modification clause.][3]

Seller: *Buyer:*

_____   _____

Elizabeth Borden-Loeb   *Gustavus Boxer*

_____   _____

Richard Loeb   *Samantha Boxer*

Date: _____

The Boxers sign the offer/contract and submit it to the Borden-Loebs. They review it, line out the $140,000 price figure, replace it with $160,000, initial it, and return it to the Boxers. This price is agreeable to the Boxers. You have them initial it (initialing limited changes like this is permissible), you make a copy of it, they give it

---

[1] See Exercise # 14.

[2] See Exercise # 29.

[3] See Chapter 10.

back to the Sellers, and a contract now exists. Several weeks later the transaction is completed, to everyone's satisfaction.[4]

---

[4]   Again, this chapter was merely intended to illustrate the drafting process. While the final contract covers some of the problems that most typically arise in the ordinary real estate transaction, there are other provisions that a blue-chip, belt-and-suspenders (leave nothing to chance) real estate transactions lawyer would want to include. This chapter was reviewed by such a lawyer, and I am indebted to my friend and colleague Professor Alan Medlin for his valuable suggestions and his appreciation of the limited purpose of this chapter.

Chapter 9
Computer Assisted Drafting

As they have done with respect to every other aspect of the practice of law, computers have revolutionized contract drafting. Today's students grew up with the computer and cannot imagine how time consuming, difficult, and expensive it was to create and revise complex contracts using only a typewriter. And before the advent of the office copier, the only available copies of the contract were the messy, hard to read *carbon copies*. Clearly, it is a different contract drafting world.

Word processors contain many features that a drafter will find extremely useful in contract drafting. These vary from program to program and no attempt will be made to describe the use of any specific function. But you should discover what they are and learn to use them. For example, the automatic paragraph numbering function allows you insert a new paragraph 2 without the necessity of then changing by hand the numbers on the remaining 97 paragraphs. It makes the changes automatically. The *mark, cut, and paste* function allows you to move provisions around quickly and accurately.

Some word processing features and stand alone programs are designed specifically to aid the drafting process.

A. Document Assembly. Many excellent document assembly programs are on the market. Some are suitable for creating any kind of contract, while others are substantive-law specific, focusing on real estate transactions, Uniform Commercial Code topics, corporate and business documents, wills and estates, and others. While the assembly aspects of these programs are very sophisticated, some of the suggested provisions are not drafted in a manner that would pass muster under the rules of good drafting style suggested in Chapter 3. But, with some judicious editing, they are usable. Eventually, you may want to purchase such a program.

One can, however, do simplified document assembly merely using the features found on most word processing programs. The lawyer who frequently drafts the same kind of document – lease agreements or employment contracts, for example – can draft (or extract from previously drafted contracts) all of the possible provisions that might be used and then store them either as macros that can be brought up with a few key strokes or in a numbered master list of provisions from which the drafter can *cut and paste* or use a merge function to create a contract containing the specific provisions that are needed for that contract. Indeed, if you do any of the boilerplate exercises in this book, once you have created a well-drafted provision, start your own master document file for use when you enter the practice of law. Regardless of what kind of contract it is, merger and no oral modification clauses will usually be about the same.

Some types of contracts will nearly always contain the same provisions, with the only differences being things like names, addresses, dates, identity of the goods or services, price, and other details that will inevitably change from contract to contract. With respect to this type of contract, the drafter can create a master document, putting a *marker* where each variable will appear – for example, *V1* could be the marker for the name of the seller, *Acme Industrials*, *V2* for the name of the buyer, *HiTech*, and so on. A separate document can then be created, providing the specific information for each variable in that particular contract. The merge function will then automatically replace *V1* wherever it appears with *Acme Industrials*.

B. Redlining. The first version of a drafted contract often functions merely as an offer to contract. The offeree will consider it and perhaps make a counteroffer in the form of a complete new draft. It is sometimes hard to spot the changes. Or, lawyers negotiating a contract on behalf of a client may sit down and make pencil changes to the document and then have those changes incorporated into the document. In both instances, it will be helpful to the parties to be able to see exactly what changes were made.

This can be done with a document comparison function called *redlining* that is available on most word processors. It will take the final version of the contract, compare it with the original or some prior version, and show all the deletions, additions, and text relocations. The following is an example of a *redlined* portion of a contract.

Assume that one party submitted a written contract proposal, the other party submitted a written counter-proposal, and the parties now want to compare the two. Text omitted from the first proposal is ~~struck through~~; text added by the counterproposal is in **bold**. There are also other ways of identifying deleted and added text, including shaded text, text in brackets, and different colored text for on-screen reviewing.

> *Mark M. Buyer (~~hereinafter referred to as~~ "Buyer") and Sue Seller (~~hereinafter referred to as~~ "Seller") agree to the following:*
>
> *1.   Seller will supply and Buyer ~~must~~ **will** purchase ~~twenty-four~~ **thirty** standard car loads of pulp wood within the next twelve months.*
>
> *2.   **Seller will supply pulpwood that is the standard shipping length of six feet and no more than 6 inches in diameter.***
>
> *~~2~~3.   Buyer will pay the prevailing market price on the date each order is placed, as determined by the Southern Pulpwood Association's Price Index~~,~~, **less a 5% discount if Buyer pays within two weeks after placing an order**.*
>
> *~~3~~4.   ~~It is Buyer's responsibility to~~ **Buyer will** arrange for Norfolk Southern to deliver empty cars to Seller's pulpwood facility in Lugoff, South Carolina,*

and to pay the cost of delivery to Buyer's paper mill in Tombigbee, Alabama.

> **5.   Seller will load the rail cars and notify Norfolk Southern that they are ready to pickup within 10 days after the empty cars arrive at Seller's facility.**

Redlining programs also typically mark portions of the text that have been moved, indicating where they came from and where the went to. And they possess a lot of other *whistles and bells* that facilitate the review and comparison of drafted documents.

C.   Readability Indices. Linguists have created several formulae for measuring the *readability* of written work. One of the most popular is the Flesch-Kincaid index, which measures readability in terms of how many years of education a person would need to be able to easily understand the writing. Some types of contracts are required by state law to achieve certain levels of readability. Insurance contracts and consumer loan agreements are frequently subject to these requirements. Under the federal Age Discrimination in Employment Act, a waiver-of-rights agreement between an employer and an individual employee must be "written in a manner calculated to be understood by such individual" (one could wish that Congress drafted its own statutes in a similar manner).

But whether required by law or not, all contracts should be easily read. The more sophisticated the parties to the contract and the more technical the substance, the higher the readability index can be. But no contract should be written that cannot be easily read by anyone other than a Ph.D in two disciplines. It is very difficult, however, to get a commercial contract below a high school degree reading level, and something in that area is acceptable.

Most major word processing programs have a feature that will generate a readability index for a document – and often provide a host of other useful drafting information, such as average sentence length, percentage of sentences that are in the passive voice, and the like. This is usually part of the grammar/style checker.

To generate a reliable readability index, you should first take out all of the non-sentence portions of the contract – headings, signature blocks, the date, and charts or graphs. The following two provisions were taken from an actual internet network access and service agreement, as found in a commercially distributed form book. The first provision was headed *2.4(b) Passwords* and the second provision was headed *2.6(a) Distribution/Uploading of Third Party Content.* These provisions contained no sub-headings.

> *Upon your enrollment as a Customer, you will select a unique e-mail password and Access Provider will assign you your own login password. For security purposes, Access Provider may occasionally change your log-in password and will notify you of such a change either through e-mail or via telephone. Customer is responsible for maintaining the confidentiality of his or her passwords and is liable for any harm resulting from disclosing or allowing disclosure of any password. Customers are not authorized to distribute their passwords to anyone, and if a Customer does so he or she remains liable to Access Provider (and any other person or entity) for any and all damages caused whether he or she knew about the actions of the person to whom such password(s) was disclosed. In addition, Access Provider will in no way be liable for any damages caused to the Customer who revealed his or her password to another nor will Access Provider be liable to any third parties who may be damages as a result of the password disclosure and for the actions of the person to whom the password was disclosed. In the event of a breach of security, Customer will remain liable for any unauthorized use of the Services until Customer notifies Access Provider by e-mail or phone.*

Customer may upload software files or otherwise distribute on the Services only information, software, photos, video, graphics, music, sounds, or other material (collectively known as Content) that is not subject to any copyright or other proprietary rights protection(collectively known as Public Domain Content), or Content in which the author has given express authorization for on-line distribution. Any copyrighted Content submitted with the consent of the owners should contain a phrase such as "Copy right owned by [insert name of owner]; used by permission." The unauthorized submission of copyrighted or other proprietary Content constitutes a breach of this Service Agreement and could subject Customer to criminal prosecution as well as personal liability for damages in a civil suit. The Customer, not Access Provider or its employees or independent contractors, are liable for all damages arising from such submission. By submitted Content to be included or uploaded to a Home Page or Web Site created by Access Provider or another entity for inclusion in the Services or by submitting such Content to any "Public Area" (i.e. those areas of the Services that are generally accessible to other Customers and non-Customers, such as Home Pages, chat rooms, message boards, and file uploads), you automatically grant, or warrant that the owner of such Content has expressly granted Access Provider the royalty free, perpetual, irrevocable, non-exclusive right and license to use, reproduce, modify, adapt, publish, translate and distribute the Content (in whole or in part) worldwide and/or to incorporate in any other works in any form, media, or technology now known or hereafter developed for the full term of any copyright that may exist in such Content.

Do you understand all of that? The two provisions have an average sentence length of 40.83 words, with four sentences per paragraph. The Flesch-Kincaid index is 16, which means you would need a college degree to understand it. Only 7% of the sentences are passive voice, which is not too bad. The sentence complexity, however, is 87 (maximum 100) and the vocabulary complexity is 54 (maximum 100). When combined with the atrocious errors of drafting style discussed in Chapter 3, the failure to put the various rights and duties of each provision into some sort of enumerated list, and the lack of any apparent internal organization make these two provisions virtually incomprehensible.

On the other hand, consider these provisions; the headings and numbers in bold were omitted when doing the analysis.

REQUIREMENTS CONTRACT

Samuel Adams, doing business as the Adams Electric Supply Company (Buyer) and Thomas Jefferson (Seller) enter into this contract for the sale of electric wire.

A. Background

1. Buyer is in the wholesale electrical supply business. He sells electrical supplies to hardware stores, building supply stores, and government agencies. Buyer has sold approximately $750,000 worth of electric wire each year for the past seven years. Buyer estimates that his demand for wire for resale will not increase or decrease more than 10% in the next five years.

2. Seller manufactures electric wire and other electrical supplies. His manufacturing capacity is far in excess of Buyer's anticipated needs.

B. *Buyer's Obligations*

Buyer will purchase from Seller all the electric wire that Buyer requires for resale. Buyer must purchase this wire by written order, indicating the gauge, quality, material, and quantity of wire.

C. *Seller's Obligations*

Upon receipt of an order from Buyer, Seller will arrange for prompt delivery by a commercial shipper to Buyer's warehouse in Longtown, South Carolina.

D. *Price and Payment*

1. Buyer will pay whatever Seller's posted price is for that type of wire at the time the order is placed, plus shipping charges. If the posted price for any order of wire is 15% or more than the posted price on the date of this contract and Seller declines to reduce the price, then Buyer may terminate the agreement.

2. Buyer will pay within 30 days after the receipt of any shipment.

E. *Duration*

Unless terminated earlier, this contract terminates in five years from the date below.

Although the subject matter of this contract is far less complex than the internet agreement above, it could have been worded in a similarly obtuse manner. Many are. In any event, these provisions have an average of 19 words per sentence, with 1.44 sentences per paragraph. The Flesch-Kincaid index is 12.78, which is certainly acceptable Only 5% of the sentences are in the passive voice. The sentence complexity is 38 (100 maximum). The vocabulary complexity is 36 (maximum 100). It is an easily understood little contract, and it would probably be perfectly adequate to cover this $3,750,000+/- transaction between two experienced businessmen dealing with each other in good faith.

All contract drafters would be advised to do a similar evaluation of their contract drafting efforts.

Chapter 10
Contract Law Dictates Contract Terms

As an example of how contract law dictates the substantive content of a contract, consider the following two problems.

A. A No Oral Modification Clause

Plasticaid, Inc., sells plastic kitchen utensils, containers, and other household goods directly to consumers through its cadre of Home Agents. These Agents get someone to invite friends and relatives to a Plasticaid Party in their home, where the Home Agent demonstrates the company's goods and takes orders for later delivery by the Home Agent. The order form, which contains the terms of the sale, bears the facsimile signature of the President of the company and provides a place for the customer to sign. Immediately above the customer signature line, the form states: "By signing this order form, you agree to purchase the goods listed above and to abide by all of the terms contained herein. ALL SALES ARE FINAL."

Recently, a customer living on a limited and fixed income ordered over $250 worth of goods. When the Home Agent went to deliver them and collect payment, the customer said she had decided that she did not want all of them. The Home Agent said, "That's OK. But we are having a contest to see who can sell the most of our new line of refrigerator containers and the contest ends this month. If you will order a set of those and pay me for what you want from the prior order, I will send the rest back." The customer agreed and promptly spent the money she saved on something else. When the Director of Sales found out about this, she terminated the Home Agent, took the originally ordered goods back to the customer, and demanded full payment. The customer refused to accept the goods or pay; indeed, she claimed he had no money to pay the full amount. The company sued.

The court, however, held that the Home Agent had actual or apparent authority to modify the contract , that what she told the customer abrogated the ALL SALES ARE FINAL language and modified the list of goods the customer was obligated to accept, and that the customer had relied on this. Plasticaid wants you to draft some language for inclusion in the order form that would prevent that from happening again.

First, first, you must recognize that the contract deals with *good*s and that it is thus governed by UCC 2-209. Under the common law, no oral modification clauses are given limited effect by the courts and are easy to circumvent. If the parties orally modify the contract and one party relies on the modification, the courts frequently say that the other party waived the right to enforce the no oral modification provision. And the courts have contrived other ways to limit the effect of NOM clauses. They do, however, have a desirable deterrent effect.

The conventional wisdom is that Section (2) of UCC 2-209 was intended to provide additional starch to the enforceability of these provisions. But, the UCC giveth and the UCC taketh away, because Section (4) says that an attempted modification *can* still operate as a waiver – although many courts now limit that to situations where there has been *reasonable* reliance on the modification. Further, Section (5) says that a modification can be retracted with respect to future performance unless the other party has relied to his or her detriment.

To forestall any claims of reasonable reliance on a Home Agent's purported waiver of the NOM clause and simultaneous oral modification of the contract, the NOM should expressly deny that the Home Agent has authority to do that. Although not all oral waiver/modification/retraction situations involving Pasticaid's form contract would result in the NOM clause being given effect, it seems that in the fact situation described in the problem Plasticaid would prevail. The attempted oral modification would be invalid and the customer would be obligated to accept and pay for all the goods. However, since this is in a form prepared by a merchant, it must be separately signed by the customer. A UCC 2-209 NOM clause might look something like this:

*§ 14. **Oral Modification Prohibited.** The terms of this written contract of sale may be modified only by another written contract that is signed by the President of Plasticaid, Inc., and you. The Home Agent does not have authority to*

> • *agree to the rescission or modification the terms of this contract,*
>
> • *waive any rights Plasticaid, Inc. has under this contract,*
>
> • *or give any assurances that are inconsistent with or in addition to the terms of this contract.*

Any mistaken reliance a Home Agent's assurances in this regard is at your own risk.

I have read this provision, understand what it says, and agree to it.

_____

Customer's Signature

This NOM clause was, of course, crafted to deal specifically with the Plasticaid situation. The following is a more generic NOM clause. It also specifically requires new consideration – which might or might not override UCC 2-209's disregard of that requirement in a sale of goods transaction:

> *The parties may not orally modify or rescind this contract. Any modification or rescission must be in another written document, signed by the parties who sign below and be supported by consideration. Any actions that either party takes in reliance on an attempted oral modification or rescission or one that is not supported by consideration are at that party's risk and the other party may subsequently enforce the contract as originally written.*

That might sound harsh and rigid. But if the parties want the liberty to orally modify their contract and are willing to suffer from the inevitable uncertainties that flow from any kind of oral contract or contract modification, then omit a NOM clause. Indeed, make specific allowance for it! That, however, would not be my advice.

B. Drafting Around UCC 2-207

Now you are ready to begin drafting on your own. Consider this problem. Before doing so, however, bear in mind that it is extremely difficult to *draft around* UCC 2-207 law. This is because the law continues to be uncertain in many respects, the courts have construed its complexities differently, and contracts professors often disagree radically and vehemently. For one view of the structure and substance of UCC 2-207, see Thomas R. Haggard, *U.C.C. 2-207: A Suggested Analysis*, 10 J.L. & Comm. 257 (1991). In any event, here is your problem.

Bill Duncan, owner of Duncan Equipment Company, builds electric generators and air compressors. He orders the various parts from several suppliers and sells the generators and compressors throughout Texas, Oklahoma, and New Mexico to both individual contractor/builders and outlet chains.

He orders the parts on a form, the content and wording of which was recommended by a trade association of which he is a member. It contains terms generally favorable to buyers. The orders that he receives for generators and compressors come in the form of letters, phone calls, and standard forms that the larger customers use for ordering equipment.

Several months ago Duncan ordered 25 Briggs and Stratton motors from Taft & Son, a wholesaler in Ohio. When they arrived, Duncan paid no attention to the printed invoice that was packed with them. He thus failed to notice that the price was $.98 higher than the price listed in the seller's catalog (which was the price he had listed on his order form) and that payment was due in 60 days, rather than the 90 days provided for on his order form). It also contained an additional term imposing a limit on the time Duncan could claim the goods were "non-conforming." He unpacked the motors and installed them in various generators and compressors.

Later, Duncan and the seller got into a dispute over the price and when it was due. Duncan finally paid the higher price, within the 60 day period, but he was plenty unhappy about it.

A few weeks later, Duncan ordered 100 gas tanks of various sizes from a manufacturer in Georgia. This time, when the tanks arrived, Duncan reviewed the shipping invoice very carefully and noted that it contained some additional terms that were not satisfactory to Duncan. He called the manufacturer, who told him that he had to accept the terms or ship the tanks back. Duncan said he would ship them back, as soon as the manufacturer sent him the money for shipping. They got into a heated argument over that, but finally agreed to split the cost of the return shipping. Duncan was even more unhappy about that.

Finally, Duncan received a sizeable order of generators from Hernandez Builders Supply Company in Santa Fe, New Mexico. It was on an H.B.S. Co. order form, but Duncan did not pay any attention to the fine print. He shipped the generators to Hernandez, now using an invoice recommended by the trade association, the terms and conditions of which were favorable to a seller. A few days later, Hernandez called and told Duncan that some of the terms on the invoice that were different from and additions to those on the order form were unacceptable. Duncan told him to ship the generators back, but Hernandez refused, claiming that they had a contract on the terms of the original order. This also made Duncan furious, but he had neither the time nor the inclination to contest the matter.

Duncan, however, has now asked if there is anything he can do to avoid getting into these situations in the future.

First, we need to do the legal analysis. Since Duncan is a merchant buying and selling goods from other merchants (presumably, all of the contractor/builders he deals with will qualify), UCC 2-207 in general and its special *merchant* provision in subsection (2) will control.

1. Duncan's Status as a Buyer

In the dispute with Taft, Duncan's order was an offer to buy. You note that it does not expressly limit acceptance to the terms of the offer, as it could have done under UCC 2-207(2)(a). Taft's shipment invoice says, *In response to your order of May 5, 2002, enclosed herewith are the motors you ordered. See reverse side for additional terms and conditions of this sale.* You conclude that this was a "definite and seasonable expression of acceptance" under UCC 2-207(1), even though it contains terms additional to and different from the terms of Duncan's order. Thus, a contract has been formed. The remaining question is what its terms are. Since both Duncan and Taft are *merchants*, Taft's additional terms (and possibly his different terms)become part of the contract under 2-207(2) unless:
● the offer expressly limits acceptance to the terms of the offer, which it didn't;
● Duncan objects, which he didn't do; or
● the acceptance terms "materially alter" the terms of the offer – and you conclude that under the caselaw in your state, the different and additional terms would not be construed as a material alteration.

Duncan was, as Taft contended, thus bound by those terms.

Turning now to what Duncan could do to prevent this in the future, you see that the *unless* clause of UCC 2-207(2) can assist him considerably. The first thing you will want to do is to add language to Duncan's order form limiting acceptance to the terms of the offer and giving advance notice of objection to deviating terms – of both the *additional* and *different* variety. In addition, it should affirmatively state that the resulting contract is under the terms of the offer only (to avoid application of the knock out rule with respect to the different terms).

But what if the seller ships the goods with a deviating invoice anyway? The *unless* clause in the offer merely prevents the additional terms from automatically becoming part of the contract; they (and different terms as well) continue to function as proposals for a modification of the contract. If Duncan accepts delivery of the goods, he runs some risk of having this construed (at least by the seller) as an acceptance of the additional or different terms, although most courts would conclude otherwise, since UCC 2-207 was intended to repudiate the common law *last shot* rule. Nevertheless, to avoid that misunderstanding, Duncan may want to add language to expressly negate that result. This can be done by stating that if the seller ships the goods or otherwise accepts the offer to buy, then a contract results under the terms of the buyer's order and the buyer's acceptance of the goods does not constitute assent to any additional or different terms. This would also prevent the invocation of UCC 2-207(3) and any possible application of the *knock out* rule, with the *different* terms canceling each other out and the term being supplied by a UCC gap filler.

Finally, what if the seller's invoice incorporates the *unless* clause of 2-207(1)? This clause prevents the purported acceptance from creating a contract if this "acceptance is expressly made conditional on assent to the additional or different terms." What then happens if the goods are shipped with an invoice containing deviating terms and that language? Duncan refuses to assent. Thus, there is no contract on the basis of the offer and acceptance. But if Duncan accepts delivery of the goods, then 2-207(3) probably kicks in, creating a contract whose terms consist of whatever the parties did mutually agree to plus the UCC gap-fillers. Thus, if Duncan and a seller disagree over a particular term, then neither Duncan's nor the seller's proposed term is part of the contract – but the UCC gap-filler term will be (the *knock-out* rule), and it may be precisely the same as the seller's term that Duncan objects to! There is probably no way to draft around this. Duncan will have to be instructed to read invoices carefully before accepting the goods and if one includes a seller's *unless* clause, to not accept the goods unless he is willing to agree to the new or different terms. Although the law would probably require the seller to bear the expense of having the goods shipped back anyway, this should also be made clear in the offer.

Exercise # 8 – Protecting a Buyer Under UCC 2-207. With all of that in mind, now draft a provision that will accomplish these results.

2. Duncan's Status as a Seller

Turning now to Duncan's problem with Hernandez, you conclude that Hernandez' order was an offer and that Duncan's shipment invoice constituted an acceptance, even though it contained additional and different terms. Since Duncan's acceptance was not expressly conditional on Herdandez' assent to these terms, a contract has been formed. But since these parties are merchants, the contract will be automatically modified by Duncan's terms unless one of the three contingencies spelled out in UCC 2-207(2) are met. You see that the offer did not expressly limit acceptance to the terms of the offer. And you conclude that Duncan's terms did not *materially alter* the existing contract. But Hernandez did give timely notification of his objection to these terms. Thus, Duncan was properly stuck with a contract on Hernandez' terms.

To protect Duncan in his role as a seller or offeree, you should include in Duncan's acceptance (the shipping invoice) the language of the *unless* clause of UCC 2-207(1). That will prevent the invoice as operating as an acceptance if it contains additional or different terms. Rather, Duncan's shipment invoice will constitute a counter-offer. If the buyer does not expressly accept those terms, then "the writings of the parties do not otherwise establish a contract." But if Duncan goes ahead and ships and the buyer accepts delivery of the goods, this may be treated as "conduct by both parties which recognizes the existence of a contract" under 2-207(3) – with the contract consisting of terms on which the parties agree plus the UCC gap fillers. But if the UCC gap filler term differs from Duncan's term or, worse yet, coincides with what the buyer originally proposed, Duncan is again stuck with a term he did not agree to. To avoid that, some sellers make the common law *last shot* rule an express contract term, so that if the buyer accepts delivery of the goods, this binds the buyer to the seller's terms – not because the law dictates this, but because the buyer has agreed that its conduct will have that effect.

Exercise # 9 – Protecting the Seller Under UCC 2-207. Draft a provision that will accomplish all of this.

Of course, if the buyer declines to assent to Duncan's terms, Duncan will probably be responsible for the cost of getting the goods shipped back. To avoid that, Duncan might want to consider sending the invoice in advance of the goods, with a provision putting the buyer on notice that a failure to object will constitute assent to the terms of the invoice. This, however, is probably impractical in the ordinary commercial context. If the transaction involves a large number of goods and enormous expenses, it will be the result of a *dickered* contract anyway, and all the differences will have been ironed out in advance. Similarly, if the buyer's offer contains language like Duncan's own, limiting acceptance to the terms of the offer, then Duncan would be well advised to specifically negotiate the terms of the sale and not rely on winning any *battle of the forms*.

On the whole, *drafting around* UCC 2-207 may be more trouble than it is worth and the contract solutions to UCC 2-207 problems may be so out of line with established commercial practice as to render them impractical. Nevertheless, if Duncan wants a contractual solution to his UCC 2-207 problems, you can provide him with at least partial relief.

PART II.
Additional Drafting Exercises

Introduction

Some of these exercises involve drafting only specific provisions. Others involve drafting or redrafting entire contracts, ranging from the very simple to the somewhat complex.

In addition to what is contained in your casebook regarding the substantive contract law that you must adhere to when drafting the following provisions and documents, you may also want to consult the following secondary authorities in connection with some of these exercises. Your professor may suggest other sources of enlightenment. It is up to you to determine if any statutory provisions, such as the UCC, should also be consulted.

- Brian Blum, *Contracts – Examples & Explanations* (2d ed. 2001) (cited as Blum).

- John D. Calamari & Joseph M. Perillo, *The Law of Contracts* (4th ed. 1998) (cited as Calamari & Perillo).

- Marvin A. Chirelstein, *Concepts and Case Analysis in the Law of Contracts* (4th ed. 2001) (cited as Chirelstein).

- E. Allan Farnsworth, *Contracts* (3d ed. 1999) (cited as Farnsworth)

- John Edward Murray, Jr., *Murray on Contracts* (4th ed. 2001) (cited as Murray).

- Claude D. Rohwer & Anthony M. Skrocki, *Contracts in a Nutshell* (5th ed. 2000) (cited as Rohwer & Skrocki).

- Restatement (Second) of Contracts (1981) (text available from several sources, cited as RS 2d).

Exercise # 10 – Acceptance; Offeror's Power to Limit Manner

The Greater Atlanta Roofers' Association has prepared a written order form that most members in the area use. Among other things, it provides that "This agreement shall become binding only upon written acceptance by the Contractor or upon commencing performance of the work." It is customary for roofers to do the work entirely on credit, being paid only after the work is completed. Thus, roofers nearly always do a credit check on potential customers. This takes from seven to ten days.

Last year, a home owner submitted an order to the Ever-Tite Roofing Company, using the standard form that the Company provided. After ten days, when the home owner had still not heard anything from Ever-Tite, he contracted with another roofer who started to work immediately. When the Ever-Tite work crew showed up the next day to start the job, they found the other roofers already at work. The home owner told Ever-Tite that he no longer desire their services.

Ever-Tite sued and the court held that the offer had not lapsed, because ten days was a reasonable time in which to do a credit check. Moreover, the court held that Ever-Tite had begun performance when it loaded the truck with its crew and the roofing materials. Thus, Ever-Tite accepted the offer before it became aware of the home owner's decision to use another roofer – which, if Ever-Tite had known, would have operated as an effective revocation of the offer.

You represent the Atlanta Landlord Association. The members of this Association own apartment buildings, rental houses, and buildings used for commercial purposes. They are frequently contracting with roofers, painters, building contractors, and others. They want you to draft a form that will better protect their interests with respect to when and how an acceptance occurs. However, they are not of one mind about what the form should say in this regard. Some want the offer to invite acceptance only by a return promise.

Others are content to allow acceptance either by return promise or the beginning of performance, but want the beginning of performance to be defined as something more than merely loading a truck with men and materials for the job and that the owner be put on actual notice of the beginning of this performance. Still others say that the promise of a roofing contractor is worthless and they do not want to be bound until the contractor actually begins performance – subject to the same definition and notification requirements indicated above. One member of the association said he had trouble with contractors starting the job and then disappearing for weeks at a time. He says he does not want to be bound until "the rascals" actually finish the job, with full power to revoke the offer until then.

Draft alternative provisions, reflecting each of these positions.

See generally, Blum, § 4.12; Calamari & Perillo, §§ 2.10, 2.15; Chirelstein, pp. 41-46; Farnsworth, §§ 3.4, 3.12, 3.22; Murray, §§ 45-47; Rohwer & Skrocki, §§ 2.9, 2.19; RS 2d §§ 30(2), 32, 45, 54, 62, 65, 68, 87, 90.

Exercise #11 – Acceptance; Offeror's Power to Limit Medium

Frito Legere, a somewhat irascible antiques dealer who thinks the world ought to conform with his notions of how things should be done, recently discovered that this is not the case. He sent another dealer a letter in which he offered to sell this dealer, who was said to be in the market for one, a late 1700s, cherry wood, gentleman's writing desk for $25,000. Believing that he was entitled to a written acceptance and that one week was more than ample time for a response, he sold the piece to someone else when the first dealer failed to respond in writing and within that time frame. A few days later (10 days after the date of his letter), the other dealer phoned Legere and purported to accept the offer. When Legere refused to sell, the other dealer sued and recovered substantial damages.

Before Legere makes any other offers of this kind, he wants to ensure that this will not happen again. Draft appropriate language to include in his offers.

See generally, Blum, § 4.12; Chirelstein, pp. 41-43; Farnsworth, § 3.13; Murray, § 45; Rohwer & Skrocki, § 2.7; RS 2d §§ 30, 65.

Exercise # 12– Advertisements

In *Lefkowitz v. Great Minneapolis Surplus Store*, 86 N.W.2d 689 (1957), the store published the following newspaper advertisements, two weeks in a row:

Saturday 9 A.M. Sharp
3 Brand New
Fur
Coats
Worth to $100.00
First Come
First Served
$1
Each

Saturday 9 A.m.
2 Brand New Pastel
Mink 3-Skin Scarfs
Selling for $89.50
Out they go
Saturday. Each $1.00
1 Black Lapin Stole
Beautiful,
worth $139.50 . . . . $1.00
First Come
First Served

Mr. Lefkowitz, who was the first person to appear at the appropriate counter of the store on each Saturday, demanded the coat and stole, and tendered $1.00 for each item. On both occasions the defendant store declined to sell Lefkowitz the goods, claiming that under a *house rule* the offer was intended for women only.

Lefkowitz sued. The store apparently defended on three grounds. (1) It contended that the offer was modified by the *house rule* mentioned above. The court rejected this defense on the grounds that the advertisement contained no such restriction. (2) The store also contended that the advertisement was a *unilateral offer* that could be withdrawn without notice. The court implicitly rejected that defense, without discussion. (3) Finally, the store argued that the advertisement was merely an invitation for offers that, when received, could be accepted or rejected – and that since Lefkowitz' offer was not accepted, no contract arose. The court, focusing on this third defense, stated that where an advertisement is "clear, definite, and explicit, and leaves nothing open for negotiation, it constitutes an offer, acceptance of which will complete the contract." The court further held that these advertisements satisfied that test.

It is now a year later. Since the original advertisements did in fact get many customers into the store, where they spent a lot of money on other items, the manager wants to repeat the promotional gimmick. But he also wants to avoid what happened in the *Lefkowitz* case. He has asked you to redraft the advertisement accordingly.

You may assume that under state law no store or other place of public accommodation may "refuse to provide goods or services to any person on the basis of that person's race, color, national origin, sex, or religion."

See generally, Blum § 4.4; Calamari & Perillo, § 2.6(e); Chirelstein 40-41; Farnsworth, § 3.10; Murray, § 34.A; Rohwer & Skrocki, § 2.3; RS 2d § 26 (and comment *b*).

Exercise # 13 – Arbitration

Rearden Steel Company, located in Atlanta, fabricates special-order steel beams, girders, and other steel products for customers throughout the entire Southeast. In recent years, Rearden has been plagued with breach-of-contract lawsuits that turned on terms-of-art in the steel fabrication business, an understanding of steel fabrication technology, and scientific proof relating to stress, load-bearing capacity, and other arcane matters. Whether litigated in state or federal court or before a judge or a jury, Rearden feels that he has often lost because the judge or jury did not understand the industry, or simply disregarded the evidence and ruled against him on a *deep pocket* theory of liability. Rearden is convinced that he will fare better if these contract disputes are arbitrated rather than litigated. Draft a provision that will accomplish that.

Exercise # 14 – Assignment and Delegation

Sarah Hudgins Simmons owns a plot of land that contains a large quantity of red-stone gravel, a very popular landscaping gravel that is, however, difficult to obtain. Harley Diggers Landscaping wants to enter into a contract with Simmons under which she will agree to excavate, sell, and deliver to him all the gravel that he requires in his business for the next five years at a fixed price.

Simmons is comfortable with that. Diggers has been in the business for many years and his requirements for this kind of gravel have remained pretty constant. With Simmons mining crew working full time, she can mine only so much gravel per month and is not inclined to try to mine more. However, she figures she can mine the amount Diggers needs at a nice profit (assuming the cost of her operation does not increase enormously during the next five years), but still be able to mine additional gravel for others and sell it at potentially higher prices if the demand increases over the next five years, as it is expected to do.

Simmons is, however, worried that Diggers either might assign his right to someone with significantly greater requirements, and thus foreclose her opportunity to sell the gravel to others at higher prices, or might assign it to someone with less requirements, thus depriving her of a fairly reliable source of income. Is her concern warranted? To be on the safe side, draft a provision that will take care of this problem for her.

Diggers, on the other hand, is concerned that Simmons might sell the land to someone who would not honor the contractual obligation. He, in turn, would be left with landscaping contracts that he could not honor. Is his concern warranted? Draft a provision that would take care of the problem for him.

See generally, Blum, § 19.3; Calamari & Perillo, §§ 18.16, 18.25-30; Farnsworth, §§ 11.4, 11.10-11; Murray, §§ 138.C, 140; Rohwer & Skrocki, ch. 12; RS 2d, §§ 168, 175-76, 317, 322.

Exercise # 15 – Attorney's Fees

Crowley Engineering Company designs and custom builds specialty equipment used in various manufacturing processes. Crowley has been the defendant in several breach of contract lawsuits in which a disgruntled customer claimed that the equipment did not work properly. Crowley prevailed in every case, but owed rather significant attorney's fees to Hudgins & Delgado, LLC. Crowley has also occasionally been forced to sue customers for non-payment – again, always successfully, but only after incurring attorney's fees. Crowley wants to include a provision in his standard contract that would require the losing party in any lawsuit under the contract to pay the party who prevails, in whole or in part, that party's attorney's fees.

Draft that provision for him.

See generally, Blum, § 18.12.3; Calamari & Perillo, § 14.35; Farnsworth, § 12.18; Murray, § 125.G; RS 2d § 356 (comment *d*).

Exercise # 16 – Choice of Law, Jurisdiction, and Venue

Alice's BBQ, a chain of BBQ restaurants in South Carolina, is owned by Alice Parker. Its principal place of business and her residence are in Camden, Kershaw County, South Carolina. She maintains direct control over all of these restaurants; each has a manager who answers directly to her.

Terry Tarheel, who resides in Charlotte, Mecklinburg County, North Carolina, and Parker have reached tentative agreement over the terms of a franchise agreement, under which Tarheel would operate several Alice's BBQ restaurants in the Charlotte area. She would not have direct control over the operation. You represent Alice and are drafting the franchise agreement on her behalf. One thing that Alice insists on is that any disputes under the franchise agreement be resolved under South Carolina law, with any lawsuits being filed in the Circuit Court of Common Pleas, Kershaw County, South Carolina.

Draft that provision.

Exercise # 17 – Conditions

a. Tom Collins is a tobacco products wholesaler. He anticipates that the United States import ban on Cuban cigars is going to be lifted in May. Collins and Rose Delight, owner of a chain of stores called Cigars Unlimited, have reached a tentative agreement under which Collins will sell Delight a certain number of boxes of Cuban cigars of various brands, types, and qualities at a certain price each month for the next twelve months, beginning in June, 2003. Collins, obviously, wants to be free of the obligation if the import ban is not lifted. Draft a provision that will accomplish this.

b. Collins is also willing to sell Delight a carton (100) of silver cigar cutters at a special discount price. Delight is interested, but is not willing to commit herself just now. Collins says that is fine, as long as she places the order by no later than June 30, 2003. Draft a provision to be included in the above contract that will allow her to do this.

c. Delight is expanding and renovating her store in Savannah, Georgia. She is planning to contract with Winston Burbank to do the work for a fixed fee. The specifications prepared by the architect call for a large, cedar-lined, humidity controlled room in which to store the cigars in bulk. Delight is a dedicated environmentalist and does not want cedar that has been cut from *old growth* strands of cedar. Udall Lumber Company is the only company that sells cedar and cedar veneer that comes exclusively from young trees that have been planted and harvested just for that purpose. There is absolutely no difference in the quality of cedar from the two sources, although the *old growth* cedar is a bit cheaper. Delight has added to the specifications the requirement that the cedar must come from Udall. Burbank says he does not care and prepared his bid using the Udall prices. Delight is going to be out of town when the work is being done and she is worried that Burbank will forget about the requirement or deliberately use the cheaper cedar, that he will install this nonconforming cedar, and that she will be stuck with it – and she knows that her actual damages for this breach will be minimal. Draft something that will help ameliorate this situation.

d. In addition to being a tobacco wholesaler, Collins also owns a few retail outlets in several parts of the country. At the present time, he does not have a retail outlet in any of the cities where Delight has her tobacco stores. She wants to keep it that way. As a part of the agreement, she is willing to pay Collins an additional $500 in return for a promise that he will not open a competing retail store for two years following the date of the contract. She want to make this an absolute duty on Collins' part, independent of her duty to buy the cigars or any breach by her of that duty. Draft an appropriate provision for inclusion in the contract.

See generally, Blum, ch. 16; Calamari & Perillo, §§ 11.1-.26;Chirelstein, pp. 108-14; Farnsworth, §§ 8.1-.4, 8.9-12, 8.15-18; Murray, §§ 99-108; Rohwer & Skrocki, §§ 8.1-.5; RS 2d §§ 24-29.

Exercise # 18 – Consequential Damages

Cooltemp manufactures window air conditioning units that it sells to various department, home supply, and appliance stores. Two of its largest customers are Highs Home and Building Supplies and T-Mart, who have agreed to buy all of their air conditioning units from Cooltemp – who, in turn, is contractually bound to supply them with all of their requirements in this regard. Both contracts provide that Cooltemp's even temporary inability to provide the necessary number of units will be deemed a material breach, justifying termination of the contract, and that Cooltemp will also be liable for any lost or reduced profits that are a result of this breach. Air compressors are a critical component of an air conditioner, and they are sometimes hard to obtain in quantity. To insure a constant supply, Cooltemp wants to enter into a requirements contract with a air compressor manufacturer.

Camden Compressors manufacturers air compressors suitable for use in window air conditioning units. It learns of Cooltemp's interest in a long-term requirements contract. Officials of the two companies meet and reach tentative agreement over the major terms. They agree to the specifications for the compressor Cooltemp needs, to some upper and lower limits on Cooltemp's requirements and to have the price fluctuate according to a certain manufacturing cost index. Beyond that, they agree to "let our people get together and work out the details."

Representing Cooltemp. Cooltemp has come to you for advice on these details. You ask a series of *what if* questions, including what would be the consequences if Camden breached the contract and failed to supply enough compressors to meet Cooltemp's needs. John Calvin, Cooltemp's vice-president, says that would be disastrous. Air compressors are hard to obtain on the open market. Even if they could replace the Camden compressors, they would undoubtedly cost more. And if they couldn't obtain an alternative supply, they would be unable to manufacture the units, they would lose profits, they would lose the lucrative contracts with Highs and T-Mart, and would be further liable for their damages.

"But," Calvin asks, "wouldn't Camden be liable to us for all those loses?" You reply that they might or they might not, and attempt to explain the rule of *Hadley v. Baxendale* (although you are not sure you thoroughly understand it yourself). In any event, you decide you need to draft a contract provision taking care of this. Do so.

Representing Camden. Assume now that Camden has come to you for advice on these details. You ask a series of questions about the factual context of this transaction, including details about both Camden's and Cooltemp's business. From John Welsey, Camden's vice president, you learn that in the past Camden has sometimes had its own difficulties in getting the raw materials and components out of which its air compressors are made. Wesley, however, knows very little about Cooltemp's business, other than the fact that it sells a lot of window units and he has seen them at both Highs and T-Mart.

Based on your experience in this area, you assume that Cooltemp probably does have supply contracts, particularly with Highs and T-Mart. And given their dominant market position and superior bargaining power, you further assume that Highs and T-Mart probably have some draconian damages provisions in their contracts with Cooltemp. You know that under UCC 2-715 Cooltemp could recover from Camden consequential damages, including "any loss resulting from general or particular requirements and needs of which the seller at the time of contracting had reason to know. . . ." Because of the uncertainty of the *had reason to know* standard and knowing that you can limit consequential damages under UCC 2-719, you decide that you had better draft a provision excluding these damages from the contract. Do so.

See generally, Blum, §§ 18.5, 18.6.2(b); Calamari & Perillo, §§ 14.5(a), 14.22; Chirelstein, pp. 179-82; Farnsworth, § 12.14; Murray, §§ 120. 125.F.1; Rohwer & Skrocki, §§ 9.2.1, 9.11.

Exercise #19 – Consideration; Exclusive Dealing Contract

Fredricka Gato is a regionally famous silhouette artist, specializing mainly in children. However, she also does pet and group silhouettes, which are quite difficult to accomplish. Gato has asked Gonzales Katz of Katz Photo Studio if he would like to become the exclusive outlet for Gato's services and thus free her of some of the administrative hassles. He would keep 30% of her fee. He told her he would like to do that and she sent him the following proposed contract:

KNOW ALL MEN BY THESE PRESENTS:

Fredericka Gato (hereinafter referred to as "Gato) and Gonzales Katz, doing business as Katz Photography Studio (hereinafter referred to as "Katz") mutually agree that for the period of one (1) year Gato will do silhouette work exclusively through Gonzales Katz' studio and Katz will be entitled to retain thirty percent (30%) of any and all fees charged.

Fredericka Gato	*Gonzales Katz*

Gato is known to be a "sharp" if not ruthless businesswoman, with a penchant for litigation if she thinks she has the slightest chance of exploiting some loophole. Katz has thus asked you to review the proposed contract and prepare a total revision that will adequately deal with all the possible problems and protect his interests.

See generally Blum, § 7.9.2; Calamari & Perillo, § 12.2(4) & (5); Chirelstein, pp. 96-104; Farnsworth, § 2.13; Murray, § 58; Rohwer & Skrocki, § 2.31.

Exercise # 20 – Consideration; Promises to Make a Gift

You are visiting with your friend, Sue Salt, an elderly widow. While you are there, Sue's sister, Mary, and her nephew, Alphonso, also drop by. In the course of the conversation, Mary tells Sue that Alphonso has just finished high school, that he graduated cum laude, that he will be going to Texas Tech University in the fall to study physics, but that their finances are pretty tight. Alphonso says he hopes he can maintain a 3.5 average in his first semester, because if he does he may be able to get a scholarship. They talk about various other things. Then Sue indicates that she has some stock she plans to sell in January of the following year and that when she gets the money from the stock sale, she wants to help Alphonso with his college expenses. Mary and Alphonso express their appreciation. Sue says, "Let's make that legal and binding." She gets out a piece of paper and writes:

> *For value received, I, Sue Salt, promise to pay my nephew Alphonso Pepper $2,000 on January 30, 2004.*

She is about to give it to Alphonso, but asks you to look at it first. "What is the 'value received'?" you ask. Sue looks puzzled and replies, "I don't know. Isn't that what promissory notes always say?" You reply that it is, but unless some value is actually given or some other form of benefit/detriment exists, the promise will be lacking in consideration and is not enforceable. She irritably asks you to write out something that will be enforceable. Do so.

See generally, Calamari & Perillo, § 4.5; Chirelstein, pp. 15-19; Farnsworth, §§ 2.4 & 2.5; Murray, §§ 56.B & 61.B; Rohwer & Skrocki, § 2.28.

Exercise # 21 – Consideration; Charitable Subscription

The Kershaw County Humane Society needs $75,000 to add a surgical and neutering wing to the shelter. It has obtained pledges covering most of that amount. The pledges read as follows:

PLEDGE

*I, _____, pledge to pay to the Kershaw
County Humane Society $_____, in*
      (1) one lump sum payment, enclosed, or
      (2) in ____ monthly payments,
*to be used for the construction of a surgical and
neutering wing to the existing Shelter.*

                                  _____
                                 Your signature

Most of the pledges were for monthly payments, spread out over two or three years. Since the Society wants to build the new facility immediately, they went to the local bank to obtain a loan, using the pledges as proof of their ability to repay. This, however, did not satisfy the bank. The loan officer said that it was highly doubtful that these pledges could be legally enforced and that the bank could not make the loan unless the Society could put up as collateral pledges that could be fully enforced as contracts.

The Society has asked you to draft such a pledge.

See generally, Blum, pp. 173, 180-81; Farnsworth, § 2.19; Murray, §§ 62, 66.A.4; Rohwer & Skrocki, § 2.41; RS 2d § 90(2).

Exercise # 22 – Consideration; Pre-Existing Duty

Carl Hubbard owns Hubbard's Nursery & Garden Supplies. For years, he has been buying his nursery stock from Jack Horner, of Horner Wholesale Nursery. They have a good relationship. Last Fall, Hubbard placed a written order for 35 Chaucer rose bushes, at $18.00 each, for delivery in the late Spring. Horner accepted the offer on a form he uses, which also contains a no-oral modification clause. Horner buys the roses from a commercial plant breeder (who supplies about 95% of this particular variety of rose to wholesalers). In the past, Horner has paid $14.00 a rose, in lots of no less than

500. Over the winter, this breeder suffered a devastating fungus among his rose cuttings, killing many of his Chaucer roses. The scarcity of the rose has thus pushed the price the breeder is going to charge wholesalers up to $20.00 each, in lots of at least 500. At that price, Horner will be taking a loss of $2.00 on each rose he sells to Hubbard.

Horner has spoken to Hubbard about the matter. Hubbard understands that these things happen, and so he is willing to agree to pay $22.00 per rose. Actually, he expects to suffer no loss, since he will resell the roses at a higher retail price. Horner's daughter, Elmira, has recently taken over most of the business and financial aspects of the nursery, leaving it to her father to look after the welfare of the plants, ensure that they are shipped properly, and otherwise attend to the horticultural aspects of the enterprise. Elmira is a very suspicious person, she doesn't know Hubbard from Adam's housecat, and she is not willing to rely on his oral assurance that he will pay the extra cost. She wants you to draft something that will bind Hubbard.

See generally, Blum, § 7.5, 13.9; Calamari & Perillo, § 4.9; Chirelstein, pp. 67-73; Farnsworth, §§ 21, 22; Murray, § 64; Rohwer & Skrocki, §§ 7.1-.3; RS 2d, § 89.

Exercise # 23 – Covenant Not to Compete

Nemo Perro is the owner of the Dura-Deck Mfg. Co, which manufactures *alternative wood* products (basically, simulated wood made out of recycled plastic and corrugated cardboard) under patents owned by Perro. These products are used for decks, docks, boardwalks, pavilions, and the like. Perro sells exclusively to building supply houses, lumber yards, large contractors who can buy in bulk, and public procurement agencies. The manufacturing plant is in Mayberry, North Carolina. Because of transportation costs, Perro's primary market is the area of North Carolina, South Carolina, Virginia, West Virginia, Kentucky, Tennessee, Alabama, and

Georgia. But he does have a few regular customers in the coastal areas of Maryland, Delaware, New Jersey, and Florida.

The product is sold by sales agents, who are assigned an exclusive territory within the primary market as described above. Agents are expected to solicit customers within the area (often, this requires several months of careful cultivation before a sale is finally made); to provide technical installation advice to both the customer and the contractor/builders who purchase the materials from them; and to otherwise promote the product within that area by attending home shows, arranging for the construction of demonstration docks and decks (where the property owner is given a huge discount in return for allowing the Perro sales agents to show the product to others), and the like.

Agents are free to work outside any of the exclusive territories and, indeed, the customers in states outside the primary market are the result of some aggressive selling by several of the agents.

Sales agents are paid on a commission-plus-expenses basis, under one year contracts – which the parties usually agree to renew, but not always. One sales agent recently decided not to renew, stating that he had obtained a better deal with Trix Wood Substitute Products, one of Perro's principal competitors. This agent had been assigned the exclusive territory of northern Alabama and had obtained some significant clients in Florida. To Perro's dismay, he later discovered that the agent took about 30% of these customers with him – they shifted to Trix products.

Perro also discovered that there was nothing in the existing employment contracts that prohibited this. Perro has now come to you for assistance. Draft a separate covenant-not-to-compete contract that Perro can offer to his remaining sales agents (and also to prospective new hires) that will prevent any of them from ever doing this. Perro says that if an agent or prospective declines to sign the new agreement, he will either not hire that person or elect not to renew the underlying employment contract at its expiration.

See generally, Blum, § 13.13.4; Calamari & Perillo, §§ 16.19-22; Farnsworth, § 5.3; Murray § 98 D & E.

Exercise # 24 – Employment Contract

The law firm of which you are a member, Corbin, Williston & Bell, LLC, is in the process of hiring a new office manager. The senior partner has asked you to take a look at the contract they had with the last office manager. The terms will remain the same, but he wants you to revise it with respect to form and style.

The existing contract is as follows (line numbering was omitted in the original). First, be prepared to do an in-class, line-by-line critique of the existing document, addressing matters of style, organization, format, and potential ambiguity (you may *assume* for the purposes of this exercise that the existing agreement substantively covers everything that this type of contract ought to cover, other than necessary housekeeping provisions – which you will need to add). Second, on the basis of that critique, redraft the contract. You may clarify certain provisions to reflect what you assume or the class has determined to be the intent of the Firm, but do not add or delete any provisions unless specifically instructed to do so.

Contract Of Employment

Know all men by these presents:

Articles of Agreement made in duplicate this ___ day of _____, 20__, by and between the law firm of Corbin, Williston & Bell, LLC (hereinafter referred to as the Firm), with offices at 647 Congress Avenue, in the City of Austin, State of Texas, United States of America, also having offices in Abilene, Lubbock, and Killeen, and _____ (hereinafter referred to as Manager), witnesseth:

That the Firm hereby employs Manager as Office Manager of the Firm for a period of three (3) years, with said employment commencing on the ____ day of _____, 20__, and ending on the ___ day of _____, 20__.

It is the duty of manager to recruit and screen applicants for secretarial positions with individual firm attorneys (who will make the ultimate hiring and termination decisions with respect to their secretaries); to recruit, screen, hire, supervise, and fire temporary secretaries as needed and one or more secretaries to be available on weekends and holidays; to recruit, screen, hire, supervise, and fire an office receptionist; to recruit, screen, hire, supervise, and fire file clerks; to recruit, screen, and recommend to the Firm hiring committee such paralegals as the Firm desires to hire; to recruit, screen, hire, supervise, and fire office runners; to recruit, screen, hire, supervise, and fire her own secretary or administrative assistant; to be in charge of ordering and arranging for the repair and replacement of all office equipment and supplies; to arrange for computer support services; to arrange for office cleaning and maintenance; to keep personnel and payroll records (including preparation of salary checks and member distribution checks, for signature by the Managing Partner, tax withholding, Social Security and Medicare withholding); to prepare checks for signature by the Managing Partner for goods and services bought or obtained; to maintain the firm books in a manner as required by the firm's CPA; to schedule vacation times for support staff so as to avoid disruption of office functions; to maintain records as needed for the administration of the Family Medical Leave Act; to maintain records as needed by the Texas Employment and Wage Payment Division; to insure that all notices required by federal or state law are posted in appropriate places; to maintain all records as required by the federal Fair Labor Standards Act; to maintain such records as are required by the federal Occupational Safety and Health Act; to recommend to the Firm's Management Committee such changes or additions she feels appropriate to the Firm's health and life insurance plans, its retirement plan, and the choice of providers of these services; to arrange for any training deemed appropriate for secretaries and other support staff; and to perform any other such duties as may from time to time be assigned to her by the Management Committee or the Managing Partner.

The Firm agrees to pay Manager $45,000 per annum, with payments on the fifteenth (15th) and last day of each month, unless either such day is a holiday or weekend, in which case Manager shall be paid on the last working day immediately preceding such day. Manager's salary payments are subject to withholding for state and federal income taxes, Social Secuirty, and Medicare.

Manager shall be covered by the Firm's health, dental, and group life insurance plans, subject to Manager's payment of that portion of the premiums required of other participants in these plans. Manager understands and agrees that the Firm may alter, change, modify, terminate, cancel, or withdraw the coverage provided by these plans, at any time without notice, for any reason or no reason at all. Manager may also participate in the firm's 401(k) plan and will withhold and send to the designatee the amount authorized by Manager and will make that deduction prior to the computation of the amount of net salary on which federal and state taxes due are based and withheld, pursuant to Paragraph 3, above.

The Firm's normal working hours are 8:30 a.m. to 5:30 p.m., Monday through Friday, and Manager is normally expected to be here during those hours. Each employee of the firm is entitled to a one (1) hour lunch break. Paid holidays include New Year's day, the Fourth (4ᵗʰ) of July, either the First (1ˢᵗ) Day of Passover or Good Friday (at each employee's option), Thanksgiving, a half (½) day on Christmas Eve and Christmas day. Employee may be expected to work overtime, including on weekends and holidays, if the needs of the Firm so require.

Manager shall be entitled to leave under the federal Family Medical Leave Act, pursuant to the Firm's policies and procedures for applying for such leave as are contained in the Firm's Family Medical Leave Act Policy and Procedure Manual, which is made a part hereto of this agreement.

During the term of this agreement, Manager may be terminated at any time for cause, including but not being limited to theft of Firm property, being intoxicated or under the influence of drugs while at work, disclosure of confidential information, sexual harassment, failure or inability to perform the duties of the job in a satisfactory manner, excessive absenteeism, excessive tardiness, refusal to follow instructions and directions, incompetence, insubordination, excessive garnishment, resume fraud, failure to adhere to any Firm policies or rules now in force or hereinafter adopted by the Management Committee, failure to maintain files and records properly, failure to dress appropriately in accordance with the Firm's dress code, breach of this contract, death, permanent disability, etc.

During the term of this agreement, Manager may be terminated if the position of Office Manager is abolished, the firm is dissolved, in the event of merger with another law firm, and for other economic or business reasons not related to employee's job performance. Manager, however, is entitled to severance pay in the amount of one half (½) of one month's salary. In addition, this contract may be unilaterally terminated by the Firm, for any reason or no reason at all, at the end of any calendar month, provided, however, that advance notice of 30 days is given and payment is made to the Manager in an amount equal to two (2) months salary in the amount set forth above. The notice of cancellation may be delivered personally or sent by registered mail to the Firm. On the service of a notice of cancellation as provided herein and the payment of the amounts due as above set forth, the Manager shall have no further rights against the company, and as part of these presents the manager hereby waives and releases the company for any and all claims and rights other than those set forth in this contract.

This contract automatically renews at the end of the contract period, unless either party provides notice no less than thirty (30) days in advance of an intent to terminate.

Manager shall be entitled to take up to three (3) days of leave without pay for personal reasons, subject to approval by the Managing Partner.

Manager is expected to follow the directions, instructions, procedures, and policies of any Shareholder lawyer with whom she works, and may be terminated for cause for failing to do so.

Each employee shall be entitled to take two (2) weeks vacation in their first three years of employment, and three (3) weeks vacation in subsequent years, but no more than two (2) weeks at a time or less than three (3) days at a time – and the timing of all such vacations shall be first approved to insure the continued and efficient operation of the Firm.

This contract automatically renews upon expiration, unless Manager indicates an intention not to renew no sooner than two (2) weeks and no longer than four (4) weeks before its expiration date.

During the life of this contract Manager warrants that she will devote all of her time and her efficient and conscientious efforts to the management of this law firm, and covenants that she will not directly or indirectly engage in or carry on any other business for her own benefit or for the benefit of any other person, firm, or corporation.

Any and all official notices required or allowed by this agreement shall be sent to the respective parties by registered mail, at the following addresses.

Corbin, Williston, & Bell
647 Congress Avenue
Austin, Texas

_____

Manager
Home Address

_____

_____

_____

Witnesseth:

William T. Bell   *Office Manager*
Managing Partner
Corbin, Williston & Bell, LLC

Dated this ___Day in the Month of _____ in the Year _____.

  Sworn and subscribed before me on the ___ Day in the Month of _____   in the Year _____.

Notary

Exercise # 25 – Firm Offer; Non-UCC

Seeing that Tommy Dwelling's house was in bad need of a new paint job, Samantha Painter offered to paint it for $750. Dwelling thought that was a pretty good price, but wanted to shop around a bit. So he asked her, "Can you give me three days to decide?" She said, "Yes, this is a firm offer and I will keep it open until Saturday noon." You live next door to Dwelling. He sees you out weeding your garden, comes over, explains the situation, and asks you to draft something that will make it "legal and binding." Draft an offer containing all the relevant details of the transaction, but structure the document and the transaction so that the offer will remain open for the indicated time period.

See generally, Blum § 5.2; Calamari & Perillo § 2.25; Chirelstein pp. 46-49; Farnsworth § 3.23; Murray §43.B; Rohwer & Skrocki, §§ 2.6-.6.1; RS 2d § 87.

Exercise # 26 – Firm Offer; UCC

Gus DeChien is a merchant dealing in pet supplies. He recently acquired at an excellent price a large quantity of nylon dog leashes made in China. He called one of his major customers, Trudy's Pet Stores, and offered to sell the leashes at $9.50 each. The purchasing agent of Trudy's said she was interested, but needed to find out how many each of her stores might require. She asked if DeChien could keep the offer open for a week. He replied that he could do that and would e-mail or FAX her something right away. He has asked you to draft an offer that will be effectively "firm."

See generally, Blum, § 5.5; Calamari & Perillo, § 2.25; Farnsworth, § 3.23; Murray, § 43.C.; Rohwer & Skrocki, § 2.6.3.

Exercise # 27 – Frustration of Purpose

In anticipation of the University of Texas baseball team defending its national championship against the University of South Carolina in Omaha, early in the 2003 season T.R. "Buck" Keeton decides that he will reserve a huge and enormously expensive recreational vehicle to transport himself, his wife, and his three children to the games, where they plan stay in a RV park. The rental fee on the RV is quite high and the dealer in Austin (a Texas A & M graduate who thinks the national championship victory was a "fluke") requires that 75% of it be paid at the time the reservation is made, with no refunds. Buck is a little hesitant, and asks you what he should do. You reply, "Well, what happens if Texas, and forgive me for even thinking this, does not make it to Omaha this year? You've got an RV with no place to go. There goes a pile of your hard earned money." Buck replies, "Durn! You're a lawyer. Can't you draft me a sneaky loophole?" You reply, "Of course I can." So, prepare something to add to the standard rental form the RV dealer uses. (P.S. Don't worry, it will not be construed as a "sneaky loophole"!)

See generally, Blum, § 15.8; Calamari & Perillo, § 13.12; Chirelstein, pp. 151-54; Farnsworth, §§ 9.7-.9; Murray, § 114; Rohwer & Skrocki, § 6.3; RS 2d § 265.

Exercise # 28 – Gap Fillers; Modification

Fritz Gutman, a retired German professor living in Dutch Fork, South Carolina, has recently gone into the business of building sun decks in the Columbia area, particularly on nearby Lake Murray. At a trade show in Charlotte, he saw some framing brackets that would be perfect for attaching the decking to the joists. The manufacturer, Holdittight, Inc., also located in Charlotte, talked Gutman into ordering 5,000 of the brackets (Gutman is very optimistic about his new decking business). The agent of Holdittight said he did not have an order form handy but wrote this out on a piece of paper:

Contract

5000 Holdittight brackets, model C5-998.

The agent then signed it,

> *William Tell, on behalf of*
> *Holdittight, Inc., Seller*

Gutman then also signed,

> *Fritz Gutman, Buyer*

When Gutman got home, he excitedly told his wife Laura Nell about this and showed her the paper. Being a far more practical person than ex-Professor Fritz, she called him a *dummkoph*! She wanted to know what the price of these marvelous brackets was, when and where they would be delivered, and what the payment terms were. He had no answers.

He has now come to you for advice. He wants to know if he is really bound to buy the 5,000 brackets and, if so, what about the missing price, delivery, and payment terms. What would you tell him?

Assuming a contract exists and that Gutman is not happy with what you told him regarding the missing terms, draft a new contract that would provide the following:
- Price – $350.00 per hundred, a price suggested by Gutman based on a posted price on another vendor's similar (but decidedly lower quality) brackets at the trade show.
- Delivery – within 10 days, to Gutman's business address in Austin, at Holdittight's expense (Gutman feels that on an order this large the seller should bear the cost of shipment, even though the industry practice is to the contrary).
- Payment – within 30 days of the completed shipment (again, a bit unusual in this trade, unless the buyer has an established relationship with the seller; otherwise, it is usually payment in advance or on delivery).

Assume that Holdittight, while protesting the outrageousness of these new terms but with a sly grin on its corporate face, indicates its assent to this new contract but then later attempts to back out. Will it be able to do that? What can you do to resolve all doubt about the enforceability of the new agreement?

See generally, Blum, §§ 7.5, 10.8.3,13.9; Chirelstein, pp. 67-73; Calamari & Perillo, §§ 2.9(b), 4.9, 5.14; Farnsworth, §§ 4.21-.22; Murray, § 38.2.-.3; Rohwer & Skrocki, §§ 2.2.1, 7.1-.3; RS 2d § 89.

Exercise # 29 – Impossibility of Performance; *Force Majeure*

Wimberly Printing Press Manufacturing Company manufactures large off-set printing presses, installs them, provides maintenance and repair service after the sale, and supplies a certain type of ink and the specially-sized rolls of paper that Wimberly presses use. Wimberly manufactures the presses on order and does not maintain an inventory.

Bill Hearst owns a chain of five small-town, weekly newspapers in western Pennsylvania and eastern Indiana – an area that is beset with heavy snow, making transportation difficult if not impossible until the roads are cleared (which has been known to take a week or more). Hearst has decided to replace all of his antiquated presses with new Wimberly presses.

Hearst has proposed a contract that sets up a January through March delivery and installation schedule under which each newspaper will be dealt with in turn. Wimberly must give Hearst at least four weeks notice of the exact delivery and installation date in a particular city. It is Hearst's responsibility to arrange for the dis-installation and removal of the old presses, a process that is estimated to take about a week. Once the old presses are out, Hearst notifies Wimberly, who then has no more than 10 days to deliver and install the presses. Hearst believes that if the schedule is met, he will not have to out-source the printing of any of the newspapers for more than three weeks – which is important to him, since out-sourcing is expensive. The contract will also obligate Wimberly to make quarterly service calls on all presses and to respond within 24 hours to any reported breakdowns. With respect to ink and paper, Wimberly will be obligated to supply these within three days of any order, for a period of three years. The proposed contract contains a *time is of the essence* clause and a liquidated damages clause that is probably about as harsh as possible (without being construed as a *penalty*).

Wimberly's manufacturing employees are represented by the Machinist Union. The current collective bargaining agreement will expire shortly, and Wimberly believes that a prolonged strike is likely over the terms of a new contract. Wimberly's drivers and service representatives are represented by the Teamsters' union.

Although their collective bargaining agreement will not expire anytime soon, Wimberly knows that if the Machinists go out on strike, the Teamsters will honor the Machinists' picket line. In addition, the Teamster employees will not cross a picket line anywhere. So, if a customer's facility is being picketed, the Wimberly drivers and service representatives will not cross it. Although Hearst newspapers are not unionized, Wimberly understands that the Federated Press Operators Union is contemplating an organizational drive among the Hearst press operators. Wimberly buys from Pine Tree Printing Products the specially-sized paper that it resells to Wimberly press owners. In the past, Pine Tree has been beset with its own labor problems, causing delays in the delivery of paper. In addition, from time to time pulp wood shortages have prevented Pine Tree from filling Wimberly's orders in a timely fashion. The machinery that Wimberly uses to fabricate Wimberly presses is itself specially manufactured, prone to breakage, and difficult to get repaired or replaced in anything like a timely fashion.

In sum, Wimberly has plenty of reasons to be worried about the strict time requirements he would be agreeing to under the proposed contract and wants you to draft a counterproposal that will take care of the problem.

See generally, Blum, § 15.7.3.d; Calamari & Perillo, § 13.19; Murray, § 112.C.4.

Exercise # 30 – Impracticability of Performance

Roque Gravel Company has a fixed-price contract with the State Highway Department to supply the gravel needed for the construction of the Highway 666 by-pass. Sam Granite owns a piece of property not far away that is rich with gravel deposits. Rosemary Roque has drafted a contract offer that she intends to present to Granite. It provides that she will mine all the gravel she requires for the Highway 666 project exclusively from Granite's property, and pay him a certain sum per ton. She has asked you to take a look at the contract.

Although Roque was apparently expecting you to review it only for form and compliance with whatever technicalities the law requires, being the good drafter that you are you go beyond that. You ask a lot of questions about the transaction, including what the price per ton was based on. Roque replies that it was based on the market value of the gravel itself; that amount, plus the cost of dry gravel removal and transportation to the site, would still give her a nice profit when she sells the gravel to the Highway Department at the agreed upon amount. You know that the water table in this part of the state is fairly high, so you ask, "What if you mine all the dry gravel that is available and the remaining gravel is below the water table?" Roque says, "Oh wow! We would have to use a dredge to remove the gravel and put the gravel through a drying process before we could deliver it. It would cost ten times as much as the dry gravel process. I would then be selling it to the Highway Department at a loss. But that land is well above the water table. So quit worrying about it."

But you don't quit worrying about it. Recalling a similar case you studied in law school, you conclude that under the doctrine of commercial impracticability, if Roque mined all the available dry gravel from the Granite property, she would probably be excused from her agreement to obtain all the remaining gravel she requires for the highway job from Granite. This would be based on the increased costs involved in extracting the gravel that is below the water table. However, you are not content with the possibility of winning a lawsuit on this issue. You decide to deal with it specifically in the contract. Do so.

See generally, Blum, § 15.7; Calamari & Perillo, §§ 13.1-.11; Chirelstein, pp. 147-58; Farnsworth, §§ 9.7-.9; Murray, § 112-13; Rohwer & Skrocki, §§6.1-.2; RS 2d § 261.

Exercise # 31 – Limitations Periods

In your jurisdiction, the statute of limitations (providing when a lawsuit must be brought) for claims alleging the breach of express or implied contract warranties is three years. Also, the cause of action accrues when a reasonable person, acting with due diligence, would have discovered the breach.

John Ross and Ira Burchenfield are negotiating a contract for the sale of certain sophisticated electronic equipment. Ross, the seller, is willing to provide generous warranties, but he wants the limitations period to be shortened. He cannot afford to have potential liability for breach of warranty hanging over his head for three years. He wants to limit it to one year, from the date of sale. Draft a provision for him.

Burchenfield, on the other hand, knows that defects in this type of equipment often do not reveal themselves until after several years of use. So, he wants the limitations period to be extended to the longer of either the statutory period or one year after the defect or breach is actually discovered. Draft a provision for him.

Exercise # 32 – Liquidated Damages

Sam Bass has decided to give up his junior partnership in the law firm of Rosemary, Sage, Parsley, and Thyme and open a hobby shop in Wilson City, Illinois, a small town 50 miles south of Chicago. Bass is an experienced modeler (airplanes, ships, railroads, rocketry, remote controlled cars and boats) and is familiar with other popular hobbies (military miniatures, lapidary, leather crafts, and the like), but he has no experience in the retail business. Wilson City does not have a hobby shop of any kind. Bass has not done a market survey of the Wilson City area. But based on information gleamed from various sources on the internet, he believes that a shop carrying the amount of merchandise he expects to carry will earn a net profit of around $70,000 per year.

Bass has leased space in the East Wilson City Shopping Mall and wants to contract with Kingman Building Contractors to do the necessary, albeit rather extensive, renovations to the space. The proposed contract will require Kingman to complete the renovations by no later than October 31st, which will give Bass just enough time to take advantage of the pre-Christmas trade – which is when hobby shops make their biggest profits. Kingman is a very busy contractor and Bass is worried that he will not be able to complete the renovations on time.

You have suggested a *time is of the essence* clause and a liquidated damages clause to "encourage" Kingman to finish on time, consisting of $400 per day that he is late, to cover Bass' lost profits. That sounds good to Bass. Draft the appropriate provisions.

See generally, Blum, § 18:11; Calamari & Perillo, §§ 14.31-.35; Chirelstein, pp. 182-84; Farnsworth, § 12.18; Murray, § 125;Rohwer & Skrocki, §§ 9.2.1, 9.5; RS 2d § 356.

Exercise # 33 – Merger Clause

You have drafted the substantive terms of a contract for the sale (by Pencils Unlimited) and purchase (by United Sporting Goods Stores, your client) of 10,000 mechanical pencils with the Atlanta Braves logo on them. The parties have discussed the transaction over the phone and in several pieces of correspondence. They appear to be in general agreement, but want a written contract to finalize it. Although they have also discussed the possibility of a doing something similar with Chicago Cubs pencils, your client tells you that they don't have an agreement on that yet. You have drafted the substantive provisions of the Braves pencil contract. Now draft a provision that will prevent this written contract from being contradicted, modified, or supplemented by any kind of prior agreement between the parties or by implied terms – in other words, a contractual version of the parol evidence rule.

See generally, Blum, § 12.7; Calamari & Perillo, §§ 3.5 & 3.6; Farnsworth, § 7.3; pp. 83-89; Murray, § 125; Rohwer & Skrocki, § 4.7.

Exercise # 34 – Mistake

Sally Port, of Port Real Estate Development, wants to buy a parcel of land in rural Raintree County, build a residential dwelling on it, and either rent or sell it. The area does not have sewage service, and so everyone in the area has a septic tank. Both the seller, Danielle Gray, and Port assume that she will be able to install a septic tank on this property as well. Unbeknownst to either seller or buyer (or you, at the time you will be drafting the contract) is the fact that running under this particular parcel is a large concrete drain that diverts water from a dip in the highway, 300 yards to the north, into Raintree Creek. The location of this drain on the property would make the installation of a regular septic tank impossible; the county would not issue a permit for such a septic tank, thus making the property unsuitable for residential use. A new form of self-contained sewage system has recently come on the market, but it is about ten times the cost of a regular septic tank system. Although this kind of tank (which is quite small) could be installed despite the presence of the drain, it is unclear whether the county would grant a permit for such a tank.

Port has asked you to draft a contract for the purchase of this land. Upon learning what she intends to use it for, you ask, "Are you sure you can install a septic tank on this property?" She replies that she has looked into it, that other homes in the general area all have septic tanks, that the land is not in a flood plane, and that the seller knows what she intends to do with the property and wouldn't try to cheat her in that regard. "But," you insist, "what if you couldn't install a septic tank because the county refused to issue the required permit, or what if you could do so only at great cost?" Annoyed with your persistence, she replies, "Well, the land would be worthless to me." This concerns you.

Assume that in this jurisdiction, the common law probably would not allow her to rescind the contract on the grounds of mutual mistake, once she discovered that a permit for a septic tank could not be granted. Hence, you decide to draft something that would cover this contingency. Do so.

See generally, Blum, §§ 15.2.2, 15.3, 15.4; Calamari & Perillo, § 9.26; Farnsworth, § 9.3; Murray, § 91.D; Rohwer & Skrocki, §§ 5.5-.5.3; 110; RS 2d § 152.

Exercise # 35 – Novation

Southern Auto Parts, a wholesaler, sells automobile parts and equipment to various retail auto parts stores. One of its principal customers is The Shade Tree Mechanic, Inc., a chain of stores spread out over the southeastern portion of the United States. They have a 10-year, renewable contract, under which Shade Tree agrees to buy certain items exclusively from Southern and Southern agrees to allow a very generous discount.

The sole owner of Southern, "Pappy" Lee O'Daniel, is now in his 70s and wants to sell the business to his son-in-law, Charlie Hayden. Pappy wants to make sure that the Shade Tree folks are taken care of, but he also wants to be free of any obligations under his supply contract with Shade Tree, which is now in the fourth year of its second 10-year contract renewal. Shade Tree is happy with that arrangement, as long as it continues to get the items it needs at the discounted prices – as is Hayden, as long as Shade Tree buys exclusively from him.

They have consulted with you. You advise that what they probably need is a novation contract. Although they don't have a clue as to what you are talking about, they trust your judgment and request that you draft one. Do so.

See generally, Calamari & Perillo, §§ 18.25, 18.26, 18.30; Farnsworth, §§ 4.24, 11.11; Murray, § 31.B; Rohwer & Skrocki, § 13.3; RS 2d § 280.

Exercise # 36 – Preliminary Negotiations; Avoiding Making an Offer

You client, Charlie Loner, who lives in New York, owns some rural property outside of Los Angeles that he wants to sell. Several weeks ago he placed an ad in the Los Angeles Times, which in relevant part read as follows: "Joshua Tree vic. 40 acres . . . need cash, will sacrifice." A few days later, he received a letter from Mark Scully, inquiring about the property. Loner wrote him back, briefly describing the property, giving directions on how to get there, stating that his rock-bottom price was $2,500 cash, and further stating that "This is a form letter." Scully then replied, indicating that he was not sure he had found the property, asking for its legal description, asking whether the land was all level or whether it included certain jutting rock hills, and suggesting a certain bank as escrow agent "should I desire to purchase the land."

Loner has now drafted but not yet sent a letter saying "From your description you have found the property"; that the named bank "is OK for escrow agent"; that the land was fairly level; giving the legal description and by then saying "If you are really interested, you will have to decide fast, as I expect to have a buyer in the next week or so." Loner really does have another buyer who is extremely interested in the property and he does not want to commit himself to selling the land to Scully just now. He has come to you for advice. Will he be bound if Scully writes back "accepting the offer"? What can he say in his letter that will prevent even the possibility of that happening?

See generally, Blum, § 4.4; Calamari & Perillo, §§ 2.5 & 2.6; Chirelstein, pp. 38-39; Farnsworth, § 3.10; Murray, § 34.B; Rohwer & Skrocki, § 2.1; RS 2d § 26.

Exercise # 37 – Proposal; Non-Binding

Charles Crowe teaches automobile mechanics and body work at the Dearborn State Technological College. He has also done a good bit of custom paint and detailing work for himself (he owns a classic 1963 Mustang) and friends. He is interested in developing this into a part-time occupation to supplement his meager teaching salary.

Donald "Pop" Duncan owns the Duncan Paint and Body Shop in Dearborn. He is anxious to retire and sell the business. Crowe found out about this. He and Duncan have discussed it and seem to be in general agreement over the basic terms. Crowe has provided you with the details of what he will pay, exactly what he is buying (land, building, tools, equipment, customer lists, good will, and the like), and other matters relating to the transaction.

Crowe wants to submit a contract proposal to Duncan, but he is not yet willing to commit himself to the deal. He still has some financing and other problems to work out, and he recently learned that another body shop, in a much better location, might come on the market soon. Nevertheless, he wants to present Duncan with a written proposal, so that each party can carefully review the details but that would not yet be binding. You have drafted a proposal (in the form of a contract) for submission to Duncan. Now, also draft something that will prevent it from being construed as an *offer* that is capable of *acceptance*, thus creating a binding *contract* – as well as prevent it from having any other legal effect.

See generally, Murray, § 31.B; Rohwer & Skrocki, § 2.1.3; RS 2d § 26.

Exercise # 38 – Promissory Estoppel; Avoidance Of

When Larry Lynn's former girlfriend, Jane Sparrow, had a baby, she initially claimed that Lynn was the father. Under state law, the natural father of a child has a duty of support. Lynn denied that he was the father and DNA tests proved him to be correct. Sparrow has now said that she is going to find out who the natural father is and make him pay support. She is very worried about how she is going to get along without that support. Lynn feels badly about the situation and wants to try to do something to help; he is not optimistic about her ability to locate the real father. He comes to you for advice. He says he is willing to pay $500 a month to help Sparrow support her son and he wants to give her something in writing to ease her worries for a least a while. But he does not want to be bound to do this indefinitely, since his situation could change.

You analyze the situation and conclude that a simple promise to pay her $500 a month would not be enforceable, for lack of consideration. However, you also know that courts have gone out of their way to enforce promises of this kind, usually relying on the doctrine of promissory estoppel. And you are worried that she might give up the search for the real father in reliance on Lynn's promise. You thus suggest that you can probably draft something that will meet his needs – provide Sparrow some modicum of assurance of help, however illusory in fact, but not binding Lynn under either contract law or the doctrine of promissory estoppel. Draft it.

See generally, Blum, §§ 8.5 & 8.6; Calamari & Perillo, §§ 6.1 & 6.2 (a); Chirelstein, pp. 22-25; Farnsworth, § 2.19; Murray, § 66; Rohwer & Skrocki, § 241; RS 2d § 90.

Exercise # 39 – Rejection of Offer/Counter-Offer; Avoiding

Peter Byrd has offered to sell Tom Cochrane a 25 foot sailboat for $14,000. Tom wants the boat very badly and considers this a fair price. Unfortunately, he is a little shy of cash and his credit at the bank is not all that good. He has written a reply that says:

> *I will buy the sailboat for $14,000, but I can give you only $2,000 right now. I will pay the remainder, $500 a month for the next two years, and you can charge me 8% interest. Is that satisfactory?*

He shows you what he has written and wants to know if it is OK. You explain to him that this would be construed as a counter-offer, since the payment term is materially different from what was in the offer. You explain that this means he has rejected the offer, that he has lost his power of acceptance, and that could not buy the sailboat on the original terms unless Byrd made him another offer.

Cochrane is not happy with that and asks why he might do. You explain that he could do one of two things. First, he could unequivocally accept the offer and then propose a modification to the contract, altering the payment terms. Byrd, of course, would not have to agree. Second, he could, without accepting the offer yet, propose a modification in the terms of the contract, but at the same time retain his right to accept the offer if Byrd refuses to agree to the modifications. Cochrane is not sure what he wants to do. While he is making up his mind, draft two provisions that would accomplish whatever he decides upon.

See generally, Calamari & Perillo, § 2.20(e); Farnsworth, § 3.20; Murray, § 42.C & .D; Rohwer & Skrocki, § 2.5.4; RS 2d § 39.

Exercise # 40 – Release

Max Pepper does not like to climb up ladders, so he hired Hector Sheba to clean out the gutters on Pepper's two-story house. Pepper supplied the ladder, which was rather old. One of the rungs broke when Sheba stepped on it, causing Sheba to fall to the ground. Sheba did not seem to be seriously hurt, but he went to Doctors-in-a-Box and they treated him for bruises, abrasions, and a strained back – at a cost of $157 .86 (including a prescription to ease the pain of the strained back). He expects to be completely recovered in a week or 10 days.

Pepper is willing to reimburse Sheba for the cost of the doctor's visit, but he wants Sheba to release him from any other claims. Draft a release for Pepper.

See generally, Calamari & Perillo, § 9.26(d); Farnsworth, § 9.2; Rohwer & Skrocki, § 5.5.2; RS 2d §§ 152 (and comment *f*), 284.

Exercise # 41 – Revocation; Preserving the Right Despite Reliance

Fenster Windows manufactures prefabricated wood and aluminum window units for both residential and commercial buildings. Fenster often supplies windows to general contractors building residential housing developments. Last year, Lake Vista Estates invited bids from general contractors to build 65 homes in the new development. Nelson Construction Company wanted to bid on the job and has invited bids from subcontractors for electrical installation, plumbing, roofing, and window units. Fenster put in a bid on the window units, which turned out to be the lowest. Without yet accepting Fenster's offer to sell the windows at that price, Nelson nevertheless relied on the quoted amount in computing its bid to Lake Vista. Lake Vista awarded the contract to Nelson, but before Nelson could contact Fenster and formally accept the Fenster's subcontract bid offer, Fenster discovered that it had miscalculated the price. Fenster immediately wired Nelson, purporting to withdraw the offer to sell at that price. Since Nelson was by then bound to Lake Vista, Nelson refused to accept Fenster's attempted revocation and purported to then accept the offer. Litigation ensued, and Fenster was held liable under a theory of detrimental reliance or promissory estoppel – with the court also rejecting the unilateral mistake argument.

Karl Fenster was outraged. He had attended the Judah P. Benjamin School of Law for one year and thought he had learned that an offer, unless it was in the form of an actual option contract supported by consideration, could always be revoked before acceptance.

Fenster now has the opportunity to bid on supplying the windows to a general contractor who is building a large public housing complex. Under a city ordinance, a general contractor's bid is irrevocable once submitted, but the ordinance does not apply to a subcontractor's bids to the general contractor. Fenster knows that the Housing Authority sometimes takes months before deciding which general contractor bid to accept. Fenster also knows that the price of his raw materials, labor, and transportation are subject to change. While the bid he made would enable him to make a profit, he might be supplying the windows at a loss three months from now. So, he wants you to draft something that will enable him to withdraw his offer prior to its actual acceptance, the doctrine of detrimental reliance and promissory estoppel to the contrary notwithstanding. Do so.

Assuming then that you represent the general contractor who receives a bid that effectively forecloses mere reliance on Fenster's bid when the general contractor is making its own bid, what could you do to protect the general contractor's interests? But what could Fenster include in his bid to counter that?

See generally, Blum, §§ 6.1-6.6; Calamari & Perillo, §§ 2.21(b), 6.3(b); Chirelstein, pp. 52-55, 62-66; Farnsworth, §§ 3.21 & 3.25; Murray, §§ 43(E) & 50; Rohwer & Skrocki, §§ 2.12-.15, 2.42; RS 2d § 87.

Exercise # 42 – A Sales Contract

Your client, Samuel Ahab, owns a 24-foot Floatbest pontoon boat that he keeps at his dock on Lake Moby. Its serial number is IR66S68932. Its South Carolina registration number is 1998-35901-C. It has a 40-horse power Juniper outboard motor, serial number 5598123359876. Its South Carolina registration number is M-1998-99876291. It is equipt with:

- a port-a-potty, that has never been used;
- a canvas top; and
- a Sonic depth/fish finder, that does not work (Ahab thinks the problem is that the sensor on the bottom of the left pontoon was damaged when the boat settled

onto the shoreline of the lake during a draw-down several years ago, but he is not sure).

The pontoons have several dents and dings in them, but Ahab thinks they are still watertight. The starter battery is old and has been recharged several times; no telling when it will go out. The motor had a major overhaul last year, but still runs rough. The seats are mold stained and have some holes in them. The carpet is shot. The muskrats have also chewed off some of the plastic covering to the steel steering cables.

Ahab owns the boat outright and title to the boat and motor is in his name. To transfer title to a new owner, the current owner only needs to sign and date the *Transfer of Title* provision on the back of the document. Ahab has also paid the current property taxes on the boat and motor and has the receipts to prove it. This is a matter of growing concern to buyers of used boats. The State will not transfer title to a boat or motor if there are unpaid taxes.

Ahab is planning to sell the boat and buy a new one. He wants to get $2,500 for the boat. He expects the buyer to take delivery at his dock, 2004 Lake Road, Lake Moby, South Carolina. He wants you to draft a contract that he can present to any prospective buyers.

Exercise # 43 – Severance

A. Allowing Severance

The Fowler Advertising Agency and the Guttenburg Book Store have agreed that Fowler will write newspaper advertising copy at a certain price, produce three television spots at a certain price per spot, and for a separate price also erect a billboard advertisement on a small piece of property owned by Guttenburg at the edge of town. You have researched the matter and concluded that a billboard on this property may violate the town zoning ordinances – although that is far from clear. You will not know for sure until Fowler/Guttenburg applies for a building permit. The parties want you to go ahead and draft a contract they can sign now, so that even if Fowler is unable to erect the billboard, the remainder of the contract will be in force. Draft an appropriate provision.

B. Disallowing Severance

The same situation as above, except that Guuttenburg believes that the billboard is the key to the whole advertising campaign. If Fowler cannot put one up, then Guttenburg wants to jettison the whole thing. Draft a provision that will accomplish that.

See generally, Calamari & Perillo, §§ 11.24, 22.6; Farnsworth, § 5.8; Murray, § 5.8; Rohwer & Skrocki, §§ 5.11.4, 8.7; RS 2d §§ 183-84.

Exercise # 44 – A "Social Contract"; Binding

Jasmine Fleming, known as "Jazz" to her friends, is the widow of Edward T. Fleming, who made millions in the commercial real estate market. Jazz is noted for her gala charity balls, dinner parties, and other social events for the rich and famous of the City. Her only son, Anthony, apparently inherited none of his mother's social graces and has been an embarrassment to his mother at many of her social events – by being crude, boorish, inappropriately attired, and drinking to excess. Since he moved out of the house upon graduation from law school, he has not been invited back to any of her parties and her security people have specific instructions to keep him out.

He attended a second-rate law school with a less then mediocre record, but, because of his mother's connections, he was able to get a job in one of the City's better law firms. The firm, however, expects its associates to bring in clients, and in the last three years the only client Tony has brought in is Big Al's Pawn Shop, on a petty zoning violation that the firm was able to take care of. The bill has not yet been paid, however – and probably never will be! The handwriting is on the wall, and even Tony can read it: produce some wealthy clients or go.

Several months ago he suggested to his mother that it would help his career if she would let him come to her parties, where he could cultivate potential clients. She vaguely agreed to this, but never acted on it. Feeling that he needs to pin his mother down with a solid written commitment, Tony drafted the following:

KNOW ALL MEN BY THESE PRESENTS:

> *In consideration for her love and affection for her son, Jasmine Fleming (hereinafter referred to as "Party of the First Part") hereby solemnly promises, covenants, and agrees to invite and allow Anthony Fleming (hereinafter referred to as "Party of the Second Party") to attend any and all balls, diners, cocktail parties, charity fund-raisers, and similar social events to which fifteen (15) or more other guests have been invited that the Party of the 1ˢᵗ Part hostesses during the next twelve (12) months.*

_____   *_____*
Jasmine Fleming   *Anthony Fleming*
Party of the First Part   *Party of the Second Part*

Dated this ___ Day in the Month of _____ in the Year _____.

Sworn and subscribed before me on the ___ Day in the Month of _____ in the Year _____.

_____
Notary

You are on the fast track to a partnership in this law firm and feel sorry for and have thus befriended poor old Tony on several occasions. He has thus asked you to take a look at his proposed contract and to revise it if you think that is necessary. Do so.

See generally, Calamari & Perillo, § 2.4; Farnsworth, § 3.7; Murray, § 31(D); Rohwer & Skrocki, § 2.1.1; RS 2d § 21 (comment *c*).

Exercise # 45 – Specific Performance

For more than 40 years, Grover Goforth has been collecting church/funeral parlor/advertising fans that date from the 1920s, 30s, and 40s. He now has over 400 rare if not one-of-a-kind fans. His is the largest private collection of these fans in the country and it would be impossible to replicate the collection on the open market. Goforth, however, has decided to sell the collection after the first of the year (for tax reasons), which is several months away yet.

The Philadelphia Museum of American History has expressed a vigorous interest in acquiring the collection, believing that the fans represent a bygone era of American social history and that the collection will enhance the Museum's reputation. The Museum and Goforth have tentatively agreed to a price of $10,000. The Museum believes this is a bargain and is worried that Goforth will get a better offer from some wealthy private collector – an offer the Museum probably could not match. So, the Museum wants to get the deal locked up. It has drafted a contract for your approval, for submission to Goforth. It is fine in every respect, except that you feel it should contain a remedies provision allowing for specific performance – that is, an order requiring Goforth to sell the fans to the Museum, even if Goforth gets a better offer from someone else and would thus be tempted to breach the contract.

Draft such a provision to be included in the contract of sale.

See generally, Blum, § 18.10; Calamari & Perillo, §§ 16.1, 16.3; Farnsworth, §§ 12.4-.7; Murray, § 127; Rohwer & Skrocki, § 9.6; RS 2d §§ 357-69.

Exercise # 46 – A Student/Professor Contract

After 30 years as an in-house attorney (specializing in labor problems, including the negotiation of the company's collective bargaining agreements with several labor unions) and for the last ten years as the General Counsel of the company, James Horatio Pike retired and has become an Adjunct Instructor of Law at the Judah P. Benjamin School of Law where he teaches, among other things, the first year course in Contracts. He also remains active as a Colonel in the Marine Reserves.

Pike's first several weeks at the school have been troublesome. Pike has complained to the Dean that his students are "lackadaisical, generally unprepared, unwilling to engage in the give and take of Socratic dialogue, unable to answer the simplest of questions about the cases, indifferent to the subject matter, irregular in attendance, often late to class, inappropriately attired, disrespectful of him, and surly when he tries to point out their reasoning and comprehension deficiencies."

On the other hand, the students have complained to the Dean that Professor Pike "is autocratic, asks impossibly complex questions, demeans and belittles students who fail to meet his expectations, is intolerant of differing points of view, sneers at case results he disagrees with, is openly biased in favor of business interests at the expense of consumers, virtually ignores the women and racial minorities in the class, gives impossibly long assignments, often fails to cover all of these materials in class, refuses to answer in-class questions and is unapproachable out of class, and has threatened to give an exam 'no one can pass' unless the students 'get with the program.'"

The Dean knows Professor Pike quite well. And he knows that today's students are different from how they were when he and Professor Pike were students together at the University of Texas School of Law back in the 60s. But he believes that both sides are vastly exaggerating the problem – which is not to say a problem does not exist. He believes that there has simply not been a *meeting of the minds* between the students and Professor Pike regarding what the reasonable expectations of each should be in this situation – a problem that the Dean believes is not unique to Professor Pike and his students.   Hence, he sees a solution in the form of a student/faculty contract.   Indeed, he would like to have one that could be used by all professors at the school.

Your instructor will assign one or more of the following variations to all or portions of the class:

1.   You have been retained by the students to draft and negotiate the terms of this contract. This will be the students' initial proposal.

2.   You have been retained by Professor Pike to draft and negotiate the terms of this contract. This will be Professor Pike's initial proposal.

3. You have been retained by the Dean to draft an objectively reasonable contract for submission to both parties and to then conduct a non-binding mediation in an effort to bring the parties into agreement.

Remember: Although the difficultly between Professor Pike and his students provides the immediate problem that the contract will resolve, it should be broad enough to encompass faculty/student relations generally at the Judah P. Benjamin School of Law (which you may assume is very much like your law school) and to deal with behaviors beyond that allegedly manifested by Professor Pike and his particular group of students.

Exercise # 47 – Third Party Beneficiaries

The Pine Tree Estates Homeowners' Association, Inc. was created by the developer of the recently completed Pine Tree Estates subdivision, Jack Spratt. The stated purpose of the Association is "to insure the continual quality of the roads, parkways, and community facilities of [the subdivision] and to otherwise act on behalf and for the benefit of the homeowners within [the subdivision]." Spratt set up the Homeowners Association in such a way that he will maintain primary control (have 51% voting rights) for 15 years, with control then passing to member-home owners in the development. Acting through Spratt, the Association intends to contract with Julie Gray, of the Green Thumb Landscaping Services, for the landscaping of the entrance area to the subdivision, the wide median that divides the central road into the subdivision, and the area around the club house (which the Association has title to). Green Thumb will agree to do the initial landscaping and maintain these areas for 10 years, for a fixed fee.

A. Creating Third Party Beneficiary Status. Obviously, the landscaping and regular maintenance is for the benefit of the homeowners in the subdivision. How well it is done will affect the property value of each home. The terms of the proposed contract between the Association and Green Thumb seem satisfactory, since they require the extensive planting of shrubs and weekly mowing, edging, trimming, and other routine maintenance. Several home owners, however, do not trust Spratt to vigorously enforce the contract. They have asked you if they could sue to enforce the contract if the Association failed to do so. You tell them that there is no clear answer to that, but you can draft a provision for inclusion in the contract that would accomplish that result. They have asked you to draft the provision, and they will ask the developer to insist that it be included in the contract with Green Thumb. Do so.

B. Denying Third Party Beneficiary Status. Assume instead that Green Thumb has come to you for advice on the original contract proposal (without the third party beneficiary provision referred to above). Despite the absence of that type of provision, one thing Green Thumb is concerned about is whether any home owner in the subdivision who was dissatisfied with Green Thumb's work could bring suit under the contract. Green Thumb wants to be answerable only to Spratt and the Association, not individual home owners. You tell them that there is no clear answer to that, but that you can draft a provision for inclusion in the contract that would make such suits impossible. Do so.

See generally, Blum, §§ 19.2.1-19.2.4; Calamari & Perillo, §§ 17.1-.4; Chirelstein, pp. 184-193; Farnsworth, §§ 10.1-.3, 10.7-.8; Murray, §§ 129, 130; Rohwer & Skrocki, §§ 11.1-.2, 11.5; RS 2d §§ 302, 311.

Exercise # 48 – Waiver; Prevention of

Nell & Nancy's Antique Mall leases space to individual vendors, usually for a full year. Under the terms of the lease, payment is due on the first of each month. An additional payment of $10 is charged for late payments made between the second and the fifteenth of each month. If a full payment (including penalty) is not made by the sixteenth of the month, Nell and Nancy may terminate the lease agreement.

Tom Goofusglass leased space for a year, beginning in January. His rent payments were paid on time in February and March. His April payment was made on the second, his May payment on the fifth, and his July payment on the seventh. He did not pay, and Nell and Nancy did not insist upon the payment of, the late fee in those months.

However, when Tom offered to pay his August rent on the fourteenth of that month, Nell and Nancy decided they had had enough and told Tom that he owed another $10. He refused to pay it, and on the sixteenth Nell and Nancy told Tom that the lease was terminated for non-payment of rent and that he had to clear out.

In an action for eviction brought by Nell and Nancy, the court held that they had waived the late payment fee provision, that they were not justified in refusing to accept his August payment, and that they thus had no right under the contract to terminate.

Nell and Nancy want you to draft a provision they can include in their future leases that will avoid this result. At the same time, they do not want to be forced to impose the penalty in every case of late payment, since some of their vendors have limited income and they think across-the-board enforcement would be harsh.

See generally, Calamari & Perillo, § 11.32; Farnsworth, § 8.5; Murray, § 89.E; Rohwer & Skrocki, §§ 7.8-.9, 8.6.4.

Exercise # 49 – Warranties; Disclaimer

Goodbody Medical Remedies sells through mail order catalogs and television advertising a variety of medical devices, including the Dr. Goodbody Muscle Pain Reliever. It is basically a battery operated heating pad that sends out low wattage and barely detectable electric impulses. It is regarded as harmless, but most doctors would strongly recommend that persons with pacemakers not use it. In its advertisements it is touted as *lasting a lifetime* and is said to be suitable for *curing muscle pain, cramps, spasms, lower back pain, sprains, and neck tension headaches.* It is also said to *help ease the pain of arthritis.* The company wants you to draft something to include in the instructions that are sold with the product that will disclaim all warranties, express or implied.

Draft such a provision.

See generally, Blum, § 10.9.2; Murray, §§ 89.F.2, 100.E.1; Rohwer & Skrocki, §§ 8.10-.10.2.

Exercise # 50 – Warranties; Express But With Limited Damages

Creative Gardens sells small (4' x 4' x 5') greenhouses made of aluminum frames and sliding glass panels on all sides. The greenhouses are shipped unassembled. To obtain a competitive advantage, the company has decided that it is willing to offer what they call a *limited lifetime warranty*. They want you to draft the warranty.

Needless to say, you are a bit uncertain as to exactly what they are willing to warrant (*e.g.,* what does the *limited* mean?), but upon further inquiry you discover that:

- They are willing to warrant against defects in the materials or workmanship, provided the greenhouse is put together properly.
- It will not cover any damage that is caused by the purchaser or any third party, such as a glass pane being broken by a baseball or the purchaser dropping it when moving it from one place to another.
- It will not cover any damage caused by the weather, such as hail or a strong wind blowing it over or sending a tree down on it.
- The original purchaser cannot transfer the warranty.
- The company will only replace the defective or broken part.
- It will not cover any damage to plants in the greenhouse, such as the loss of a rare orchid when a pane broke and the flower froze, or injury to the owner, such as injury caused by broken glass.

Draft the warranty provision for the company.

See generally, Murray, §§ 96.B.2.e, 100.B, 100.E.3.